Windy Road
My Journey from Horseback to Helicopter and Home

Windy Road
My Journey from Horseback to Helicopter and Home

Dennis L. Kaltreider

Copyright © 2020 Dennis L. Kaltreider
All rights reserved.
ISBN: 978-0-9854819-3-3

DEDICATION

To my brothers and sisters in arms, especially the 57,939 who gave their lives, the ultimate full measure of sacrifice and devotion.

To the men and women who continue to suffer from the painful physical and emotional effects of their service. My heart also goes out to their families for their enduring sacrifices.

To the nearly 1600 individuals still missing or unaccounted for.

To our Vietnamese brothers and sisters who suffered similar fates in this war.

To all who served, may their contributions be respectfully honored.

CONTENTS

	Acknowledgments	iii
	Introduction	v
	Author's Note	vii
1	Two	1
2	Unchained Melody	5
3	Where Have All the Flowers Gone?	23
4	Leaving on a Jet Plane	27
5	500 Miles	33
6	A Hundred Pounds of Clay	37
7	The Times They Are a-Changin'	43
8	We Gotta Get Outta This Place	53
9	Twist and Shout	59
10	My Girl	67
11	Baby I Need Your Lovin'	73
12	What's Your Name?	77
13	(I Can't Get No) Satisfaction	91
14	Mr. Tambourine Man	97
15	Dedicated to the One I Love	103
16	If I Had a Hammer	115
17	Ticket to Ride	119
18	King of the Road	123
19	House of the Rising Sun	127
20	Cupid (Draw Back Your Bow)	129
21	My Windy Road	131
	Postscript	135
	Appendix	139

ACKNOWLEDGMENTS

To close friends and my military family with whom I've maintained contact over the years, I extend my grateful appreciation for helping me clear some of the cobwebs of my muddled mind and addled memory.

Jeff Young and Ron Gingerich, my two closest friends from high school, endured their own difficult journeys in Vietnam and long after. Both of them have encouraged and supported me beyond measure. Frank Swegheimer, my barracks roommate for part of the time in Pleiku, continues to be a steadfast friend and confidant, a reminder of some of the good friends I did make in those troubling times. "Monterey Jack" Mahan, a "brother" from C Company, 43rd Signal Battalion, helped to clarify and fill in details about some of the blank pages that have tormented the fragmentary chronicles in my mind. Bill Comrey, another HHD pal, 43rd Signal Battalion, has helped rebuild some of the visual pieces of this jumbled puzzle and has assisted me in reconnecting with many of my fellow Vietnam veterans. Indeed, I salute all the individuals from 43rd Signal Battalion, 21st Signal Group, 1st Signal Brigade and other units with whom I served and/or shared these life-changing experiences.

Most of all, my sincere thanks and gratitude go to my dear wife Lynne Warfield Kaltreider who has stood by me in war and peace, injuries and health for more than half a century. Her love can never be measured or matched.

INTRODUCTION

Năm Con Khỉ và Sự kiện Tết Mậu Thân 1968

It was the start of the Year of the Monkey and the Vietnamese Lunar New Year, a time of anticipated calm and celebration. But there was no calm and we were not celebrating.

At 2:00 am on January 30, 1968, we suddenly came under an intense rocket and mortar attack. In fact, within a few hours and during the course of the next few days, the entire country -- from major cities to small towns and every military base in between -- came under fierce, highly coordinated attacks by the Viet Cong and forces of the North Vietnamese Army.

It made perfect sense that I did not have time to write to my wife, Lynne. And when I finally caught a moment's break several days into the offensive, I did write. But I did not mention the fighting, the whistling rockets, or the reverberating mortar explosions in and around our compound. I did not tell her about the tense and nerve-wracking moments spent staring into the impenetrable darkness, the blackest hours of night when most of the attacks on our compound occurred. I did not explain the futility of trying to see some vestige of a mysterious enemy creeping through the grass outside our perimeter or crawling through hand-dug tunnels just outside "the wire" and up to the edge of our compound.

Instead, I wrote two notes. One was a brief letter about our formative relationship. The second was a poem that, like many of my more creative endeavors, carried me to simpler, perhaps more idealized times. This note of expressive verse conveyed something I lacked before November 9, 1966, the evening when Lynne and I met for the first time. Perhaps as important, this impassioned writing transported me from this frightening and perilous situation I suddenly had been thrust into, to a safer and more reassuring place. Writing reflective love letters and poetry was one of my ways of coping with a foreboding, ever-present, and threatening unknown. I also believe it was my way of trying to protect her from the grim and menacing reality of the war in which I was now becoming fully immersed.

"Spring Mill"

*In Spring I used to sit and watch
The water flow the gauntlet there
And hear the drip of melted snow
On mossy rocks.
I sat in wind and rain and sun
And - strange - I never tired of it,
But stayed for hours, end on end
To wait and look.
A time when croci hadn't gone
But early blossoms did peek thru
And frost did chill the morning air
Once in a while.
The years I had then were but few.
But smiles in number kissed my lips
And glowed upon the ear of friends
Who passed nearby.
The stream that never-ending ran
Too, smiled its song I yearned to know,
And whispered soft and spoke aloud —
A wondrous feast.
The slip of oars in water clear —
Its brush with talent, portraits drew
Beneath the shade of sculptured bank
Circles rounding.*

*Now just a little further o'er
The millrace and the water wheel
Stood, working every hour of time
Around the clock.
Never did I see that wheel pause.
It was perpetual, never ceasing.
And its thirst was always the same
Insatiable.
It was - as it never could drink
enough to satisfy itself
and the wheels and cogs that inside
creaked, grunted, sighed.
The miller often stepped outside
To look upon his turning wheel
And waved to me across the still, almost quiet pond.
How my smiles increased!
To wave back
Was a joy almost as great as
Weaving a garland of daisies
For one I love.
Love - a wondrous feast.
The joy of Sharing everything in one's life;
The joy of giving everything
To one you love.*

For Lynne - All my love - my life entire.

February 3, 1968

AUTHOR'S NOTE

Music has always been an integral part of my life and has played a significant role in many things I continue to do. From the time I could recognize and hum along to tunes on my parents' kitchen radio, I was listening, singing, creating, and eventually performing music in many genres and in a variety of places. As you'll read later, even in the midst of the tumult and struggles of my Vietnam experience, music sustained me through unsettled, sometimes boring nights. It provided a temporary outlet that allowed me to escape the sometimes surprisingly mundane, albeit menacing and worse yet, deadly reality of this confusing, convoluted conflict.

Every chapter in this book has a song title that relates to the chapter in some way. All of these songs were ones I included in my performances at a handful of venues during my 3 years in the Army, most notably at gigs in NCO Clubs in the Central Highlands of Vietnam. These frequently requested tunes are listed by title and the performer whose version is usually recognized or credited with making it famous. Beneath the title, I cite the writer and the date it was written or copyrighted or the year it reached its peak on record charts.

Specific dates are printed in bold and included to help make sense of the chronology of this odyssey. The body of this book is printed in Palatino (font) with words in italics representing direct quotes from the more than 250 letters I wrote to Lynne while I was at Fort Knox and in Vietnam. In some cases, excerpts from news articles I wrote also are italicized and noted as such. Fanciful or quaint spellings and my use of uncommon words like *thee* and *thou, tho* or *brite* have been left unchanged in these directly transcribed quotes. They are included to illustrate the poetic license I employed in my ardent writing to her.

Indented text beneath a date (in *Arial Narrow Italic* font) are specific quotes from the 230+ letters which Lynne wrote to me, as well as some notes a few other people sent to me while I was in Vietnam.

Information listing the identity of specific enemy units along with many other statistics I cite are all from declassified documents including those revealed in a Top Secret-UMBRA report "Declassified and approved for release by NSA 12-18-2018 pursuant to E.O. 13526."

Chapter One

"Two"
Denny Kaltreider
(Written by Denny Kaltreider - 1966)

I was frustrated and angry with the local Selective Service "Draft Board" in my hometown of York, PA. I recently had completed 2-years' service to my country as a Peace Corps Volunteer in Colombia, South America, plus an additional two months as a Peace Corps Field Coordinator and Trainer for prospective volunteers at Brandeis University in Waltham, MA. I was ready now; I was physically, emotionally, and mentally prepared to continue my formal schooling. So, in September 1966, I began attending classes at the University Park Campus of Penn State University. Then, without warning, I received a letter with the odious "Greetings" salutation and the universally dreaded "Order to Report" notice. I was about to be drafted.

And so, only a few weeks into my first semester at Penn State, I was forced to pause my studies and reluctantly return home to York. There, I pleaded my case in person to the board and appealed to them for a 2-S, Educational Deferment. I explained to them how I had served my country and now wanted to continue my education.

Their immediate response? A curt, "No way. You're just trying to evade the draft by trying to go to college."

When I brought up the fact that I was being treated for a positive PPD test (a test for exposure to tuberculosis from my time in South America) and that I was on a strict, daily pill regimen, their sarcastic response was something along the lines of ... "You'll be able to take them. You'll have access to water. The Army will give you a canteen."

Their disparaging cynicism was not lost on me.

I was dumbfounded and overwhelmingly discouraged. At that point, my only alternative would have been profoundly drastic; I could leave the country and become an expatriate. While some young men chose to do that and simply moved to Canada to avoid being drafted, I was not prepared to take that desperate measure. I did not want to leave my home again, especially with no assurance I could ever return. So, what to do?

I went back to Penn State to pack my belongings and to say goodbye to two of my best friends, Jeff Young and Dianne Field, high school classmates who were already in their junior year.

In mid-October 1966, shortly before my 21st birthday, I reported for my pre-induction physical at Olmstead Air Force Base near Middletown, PA.

At the end of my testing I had a conversation with several of the lab technicians about the two years I had spent in my very recently completed, life-changing, South American adventure. I told them about my first year of Community Development work just north of the Amazon in the isolated village of Nilo, Cundinamarca, Colombia. Likewise, I described my second-year's work in the capital city of Bogotá, Colombia as an illustrator for the Colombian Educational Television series, *El Lorito Profesor*.

The specific comments of that conversation are impossible to recall, but I'm sure I expressed trepidation at the thought of potentially becoming "just another piece of cannon fodder in Vietnam."

Someone suggested (as recruiters apparently do to every "newbie"), that a different approach might possibly be a viable alternative for me. Said one of the technicians, "You know, you could enlist. Then you'd have at least some chance of requesting training in a particular MOS (Military Occupational Specialty), something other than just being a grunt (slang for foot soldier). And then you also could apply to OCS (Officer Candidate School)."

A myriad of thoughts raced through my mind. I felt I had matured significantly, especially when contrasted with many young men my age. I had learned to take control over many parts of my life, yet, now it seemed I was about to lose so much of that. The thought of retaining at least some control was immediately appealing.

Consequently, I made the decision right then and there that the inflexible, cut and dried attitudes of insensitive people on the Draft Board would not be the ones to determine my future. Damn it, I would control my own destiny! So, immediately after my physical, instead of being "drafted," I jumped the proverbial gun and enlisted for three years in the US Army.

I was scheduled to depart for Basic Training at Fort Knox, KY, on October 31, 1966, but as I prepared to say goodbye to my family, I received a curious surprise – a notice that my training had been delayed for two full weeks. I was told to remain at home and report to Fort Knox on Nov 12-13. Apparently, the Army "didn't have room" for a new training group at Fort Knox so my three years in the Army would begin at home! This unexpected pause at the start of a new and quite unimaginable experience would prove to be more fortuitous than I could ever imagine.

Tuesday & Wednesday, November 8 & 9, 1966

I dilly-dallied around my hometown for the next several days, then drove to Penn State for the weekend with a friend, Jane March. We attended the Homecoming football game against Syracuse, and a concert in Rec Hall by the "Supremes." I returned to York and ended up during one of my last evenings home at the *Hawks Gunning Club* in Pleasureville. The Hawks Club was (and still is) a bar and private social club about half a block up a side street from where my parents lived.

On November 8, 1966, the day after my 21st birthday, I was having dinner at the Hawks Club bar, when I bumped into Dave Bahn, a good friend from high school. We reminisced over a few cold beers and then made plans to meet again the following night, November 9. We decided to make an unannounced visit to one of our all-time favorite teachers, Arthur Edwin Warfield, our former high school music teacher. Mr. Warfield had corresponded with me several times during my time in South America and I personally wanted to say "farewell" once again as I began this new odyssey.

Dave and I drove to Wrightsville, a small town located on the west bank of the Susquehanna River, south of Harrisburg. We parked on the street in front of the house, climbed the few porch steps to the door of 123 N. Fourth Street, and rang the bell. An alluring young woman opened the door.

Thinking quickly, I said, "You must be Lynne." Even though she and I had never met, her father had mentioned her name several times in the letters he wrote to me while I was working with the Peace Corps in South America. Lynne had graduated from college and now was living with her parents and working in Harrisburg.

After we introduced ourselves, she invited us in and we spent a wonderful evening of conversation, laughter, and music. Lynne and her father took turns playing the beautiful Steinway grand piano in their living room and we all joined in singing along. Lynne's father invited me back for lunch the following day. And I reciprocated by asking Lynne to come to my parents' home for dinner two days later. Thus, the magic began. I was overwhelmingly smitten by this charming, intelligent, and talented young woman. But, alas, I still had to leave for Basic Training in just a few days.

Lynne and I both were beguiled and seduced by this serendipitous meeting, the enchanted evening, and the intriguing joy-filled days that followed. Yet neither of us was sure what might be happening or, indeed, if this was just a random, enigmatic, one-time event. So, we simply said, "Good-Bye" and parted with a less-than-convincing promise that we'd write.

Chapter Two

"Unchained Melody"
The Righteous Brothers; other artists
(Written by Alex North and Hy Zaret - 1955)

An olive drab blur filled with loud voices and monotonous repetition is the essence of what I recall from my first days at the Fort Knox Reception Station; the rest is lost to history. Still, one of the aspects that remains steadfastly ingrained in my mind is quite similar to stereotypic scenes portrayed in movies. That is, the litany of non-stop badgering from the DIs (Drill Instructors), endless slogging through dull and menial tasks, the drudgery of repetitive fundamental drills -- march, march, march -- left face, right face, about face, halt -- march, march, march — over and over and over. No weapon to carry with the proverbial commands, "left shoulder," "right shoulder," "port arms." No, we just marched, marched, marched, "learning" how to move in synchronization as a unit. And, I recall one other inconsolable element, the uncommonly quiet, lonely, boring nights.

I penned my first letter to Lynne on Armor Center stationery, on **November 19, 1966**. The five page missive of news and some falderol began, *"I've been thinking about writing ever since I arrived, every time the thought of it came up I put it off, thinking that I'd write as soon as I knew where I could receive mail."*

Actual Basic Training (BCT) had not yet begun for us. Neither was it clear whether we actually would undergo our Basic Training right there at Fort Knox or be transported to a different post. Rumors were constantly circulating, including one that said we might be shipped all the way across the states to the West Coast for training.

"However, we haven't shipped out of the Reception Station yet — we were almost sent to Colorado, California, and then North Carolina. But our orders never came through. I think now that it's fairly certain we'll go through our BCT right here. I won't complain."

Later in the letter I switched from what I described to Lynne as my *"Simple America"* style writing, the normal way people conduct everyday conversations and compose letters, to a more creative and expressively poetic, stylized form.

"If it exists here, it is suppressed. It can only be a glance. (If one blinks an eye, it's gone.) In other places I felt it not in death alone, but in all things. My hands thrusted (sic) *into damp, rich earth, helped to build — perhaps lives — I know not."*

"I have fondled life and its infancy. I've touched the edge of existence and love has come close to a being that wants just that. I hope I'm not wrong. I had been infatuated. I was only right in one sense .... <u>some</u> thoughts had been <u>shared</u>, many things left unsaid. Too many feelings were hidden."

"Now I have ventured even farther into the darkness that may soon engulf some part of my world. If it's rite this time ...... so much more has to be said. I have found one ember barely glowing, beginning to shine, just a tiny bit more. Time <u>can</u> fan that flame; understanding <u>will</u> feed it. Wholly I pray for a few seconds more."

"Is music playing?" "Is a voice speaking?" "Am I again mistaken..."

"It seems that I am irrational. But in that I find my only peace for the moment. I hope I don't fail."

"One last note. You cannot imagine even in the smallest sense what my last few nights in York meant."

"Before the word was exhaustion -—- now it is hope."

I was struggling with what to say, how to say it, how to express my emotional anxiety and confusion. My life had gone from incredibly free autonomy, especially during my last few months in Colombia when I was driving and/or flying from Bogotá to Medellín and Barranquilla while writing, producing, and directing a documentary about the Peace Corps Literacy Program for Educational Television. Things suddenly were flipped and I found I was the one *being directed* in every aspect of my life, including when to eat, when to sleep, even when to use the bathroom!

On Thanksgiving 1966 I began my second letter to Lynne with a very unusual introduction -- a greeting written in Arabic.

You see, there was an immigrant, student--draftee from Jordan named Abdullah (regrettably, I do not recall his last name.) Most of the guys in our barracks either simply ignored him or gave him the proverbial cold shoulder. They wanted nothing to do with him. But that was not how I treated him. In fact, Abdullah and I became friends during the short time we trained together at Fort Knox. Perhaps it grew out of my empathy for this "outsider" and my own relatively similar experience as an outsider at the very beginning of my Peace Corps tour in South America. Being in that situation elicits a sense of detachment; feeling very much alone – even lost - in a foreign country; and initially, frustration at being able to converse with only simple phrases.

One day, I was called out of formation at Fort Knox, taken to a small room in the barracks, and interviewed by a Captain from Army Intelligence. He wanted to know if Abdullah was trustworthy, loyal, etc. I had no reason to believe otherwise; I honestly felt he was fit and prepared to serve in the US Army. In fact, he appeared to be more committed to serving than a handful of the guys in our unit…especially the one disgruntled malcontent who went AWOL during our second week of training!

I did not discuss the interview with Abdullah. Later, on Thanksgiving, I asked him to write an "introduction" to Lynne in Arabic and he did. (I had no way of knowing exactly what he wrote. And even though Lynne kept his handwritten note with the letters I wrote to her, and I've checked with numerous resources, we've never succeeded in having the note translated.)

I continued my own message to Lynne beneath his … *"Needless to say, altho we had turkey and all the trimmings, etc. today, I can't help but remember Thanksgiving 1964 and 1965. They say one shouldn't become nostalgic or at least they should try to avoid it and not look back, but as I might have said before, only in that can I find any solace — only in that can I find a glimmer of hope."*

"….. I'm in a fairly good mood for the first time since I arrived. Reasons? First, I'm tired — I have been working and if I'm busy there's little time for being sad. ¿Non?" You see, I've been appointed (acting) Corporal, Squad Leader for #4, Second Platoon, D Company, 19th Brigade, 5th Battalion. So, from 4:45 am until 11 pm, I shout, scream, whisper a little at my squad. More on this later."

"Second, I may be coming home the 17th or 18th of December and I know that is keeping my spirits up a bit."

"Third, I finally finished that little song I was trying to write lyrics to when I was at your home. A copy of the lyrics is included."

The song was called "A Walk in the Fall." And, once again, focusing on music and creative writing took me away from the harsh reality of what the Army was trying to do to all of us.

"Basic" was very much like what you see portrayed or described in other media -- with "spit and polish;" that is, a little spit and a lot of polish mixed in with plenty of sweat. Loud, bellicose Drill Sergeants bullied recruits incessantly. They especially directed their taunting and mocking at any recruit who stumbled or fell behind or failed to finish any task to their virtually unattainable satisfaction. A few grizzled veterans in the Training Cadre had their own special and important role to play, teaching valuable combat survival skills. A few of them actually were battle-tested advisors who more quietly mentored some recruits (myself included) by taking them under their wings. We also had our share of a few fresh-out-of-OCS "butter bars" (Second Lieutenants) who thought they were God's gift to the Army, strutting about like proud turkeys, barking out orders in their high pitched, canary-like voices. Many, but certainly not all, of these untested and demonstrably inept individuals tried to belittle, demean, and discourage us while supposedly trying to mold, toughen, and discipline raw recruits into virtual killing machines. I often felt that they were more than overcompensating for what they had endured in their quest to become officers. Nonetheless, I wasn't really buying what they were selling, but I played "the part" of determined and compliant recruit as best I could … just in order to survive.

Beneath my compliant exterior I was seething with emotional turmoil. I had lived and worked for more than two years truly as an "instrument of peace," striving to help markedly less fortunate, sometimes destitute people both in the tropic countryside and in the capital city of an underdeveloped nation. Now someone was trying to change my demeanor and my ambition by forcing me into doing exactly the opposite. These "Regular Army" aka "Lifers" were doing their best to teach hate, to overcome and to control by brute force, and ultimately, to kill other human beings. I vividly remember bayonet drills with Drill Sergeants demanding that we repeatedly thrust full force at lifeless, hanging dummies, all the while screaming at the top of our voices, "Kill! Kill! Kill!" Everything we were being forced to do or cajoled into was in stark contrast and opposition to the peace-oriented life I had been leading.

The Army drafted 382,010 young men in 1966 according to Federal Selective Service records. This diverse and sundry assemblage came in every size imaginable - from "Lumpy, Bumpy, Chubby, Tub O'Lard" to one young man in our unit, "Chiseled and Fit" Pvt Matthews, a "hard case" from the ghetto who could run a mile as fast as a gazelle. Our Barracks Sergeant liked to place substantial money bets with other Barracks Sergeants then challenge their top runners in a race against Matthews. I don't recall him ever losing.

In addition, the recruits represented every kind of character you can imagine—like the Kentucky kid, fresh out of the mountains, maybe his first time in the "big city," who carelessly demonstrated a completely out-of-line behavior. Lying on his bunk one day, he called out to us with his Southern drawl, "Hey, y'all, look a 'diss. Ain't 'diss funny? Hooo, hooo. Somebody bin climbin' up de walls," whereupon he began to stamp prints from his muddy boots on the pristine side walls. Then he stood up and continued making "tracks" towards the ceiling of the barracks.

Several barracks mates quickly jumped in and tangibly "persuaded" him to clean up his act before the Barracks Sergeant caught wind of it.

One or two of the guys in our barracks had been drafted while still in college -- or immediately following their graduation. There were kids fresh out of high school and a couple of slightly older guys, most of whom were very much out of shape. Fortunately, I was in reasonably good shape from my Peace Corps Training and my time playing soccer in South America, so I was able to withstand the rigors of BCT reasonably well. Nearly all of us eventually would achieve an improved level of fitness in the eight weeks of Boot Camp. Those who didn't were sent to "Motivation Platoon." And the word was you did not want to be sent there under any circumstances!

---0---

Lynne's and my newly found kismet held for us during Christmas holidays as my training group was given two weeks' leave between December 18, 1966, and January 1, 1967. However, the holidays didn't exactly start out with all things "merry and bright." My bus from Fort Knox to Harrisburg, PA, was scheduled to arrive at 8:00 am on the 18th of December, but a kind Greyhound driver said I should not make the transfer in Cincinnati as the terminal staff had scheduled, but just stay on his bus and he'd get me home faster. Indeed, he did. I arrived nearly three and a half hours early, around 4:30 am, while it was still pitch dark. I found the nearest pay phone on a wall outside the still-shuttered terminal and called Lynne's home number, not realizing the "upstairs phone" was right next to her mother's bed on the 2nd floor. (This was long before the invention of personal cell phones.) Lynne's mother answered and then reluctantly called out to her on the 3rd floor. I could hear her mother's reasonably stern admonition, even though she had partially covered the phone's mouthpiece with her hand to muffle the sound, "You're not driving to Harrisburg to pick anyone up at this hour!" Nevertheless, Lynne chose not to follow her mother's directive and drove the half-hour trip to the bus terminal to pick me up regardless of the darkness or time of day.

Lynne and I spent nearly all our waking moments together during those precious days in York and Wrightsville, walking on snow-covered streets, sharing secrets and wishes, and trying to decipher just what we had stumbled across in our chance meeting only a month before. She slept in her bedroom on the third floor while I slept on the floor of their living room just so I could be close -- even though my parents lived only 11 miles away. We simply did not want to spend a moment apart.

All too soon the holiday ended ... but, I'm happy to say on a much more "merry and bright" note than it had begun. As Lynne and I began backing out of the parking space for the drive to the bus terminal and my return to Fort Knox, Lynne's mother stepped up to the rail on the front porch and waved, then called out, "You may phone us at 4:30 am anytime you like!" Score one for love! (Remarkably, I still get happy goosebumps thinking about that special moment.)

I returned to Fort Knox with a more positive attitude and a newfound desire to succeed. And I literally compelled myself to excel in all the areas I could, especially in keeping physically fit.

January 4, 1967

"Small note: Every night I do exercises after lights out. I don't have to. It's not a regulation, but there is a burning in my heart — I am not with you and so with every push-up or sit-up or whatever exercise I say to myself, "This is for Lynne." ... after a tiring day, exercises hurt. But the more I do the more I know that someday we shall be together and that tho we may hurt sometimes, we forever shall be happy."

"1. I cried a lot today. We were in the gas chambers 3 times - once with chlorine, one time with tear gas, and a third time with chlorine and something else (I forgot the name.)"

"2. I thought (think) a lot about you every day. Can't get you off my mind."

Two days later, January 6, 1967, I reminisced in a note about our Christmas together:

"Not one day passes that I don't awake thinking of a tiny doll in a small town, near a river, a few blocks from a bridge, white house filled with laughter, eggnog, Piels [beer], music, love, friendship, burned popcorn, a C-mas tree, a stone statue; a green car with dirty ashtray, paintings; old-dried-out chestnuts (bet you forgot about that!), tinsel, a star out front - facing the "frozen" river [the Susquehanna River was just 4 blocks from her home], *cats, cookies, mints, touches, candles, friends, family, ones loved, ones loving, happiness, contentment, peace, and a broken telephone."*

"Feelings cannot flow from my hand — yet, from my heart they do. Every second a pang of hurt because I am not near....... if only I could let you know."
"To touch, to see, to hear, to be with (I have to have those dangling participles operated on)."

"Perhaps tomorrow. You know, it is only ours."

"P.S. Enclosed please find one autograph from Cassius Clay. I won it in a poker game."

January 9, 1967

"The only fear I have is of losing someone very dear to me. I had no idea when I went home at Christmas that, what I had hoped to be a nice friendship would

turn about and blossom into something even more beautiful than a delicate rosebud about to bloom. 'Happiness is someone to laugh and cry with.'"

"We together shall not wish away the past, but rather, we together shall try to be patient, hope for a brite future, laugh and cry, weep sweet and bitter tears, laugh in honey colored tones and blue hues."

"I do not understand all of your plight — I have only just begun to understand my own look at a small part of life. Tho I am human and fallible, I shall try to comprehend, to have patience, to continue to make you happy. If it means I must cry openly — I shall do it. If it means I must laugh — I will do it without reserve."

January 19, 1967

"We've been out in the field for two days and have now returned, haggard, weary, tired. I've had only 4 hours sleep in the past 3 days (on tactical maneuvers) and my back is like a hot iron on plastic. I should report to sick call ... but I must go on."

I began to consider what might come next. I was completely bewildered about what the future might hold and if I might be able to change my initial enlistment commitment. I was unsure about what was happening to me and indecisive about what I might be doing if I continued this route - both in the military and in my quickened and newly animated personal life.

During BCT we underwent extensive training with several weapons, most notably the Army's standard issue (until 1970) M-14, 7.62 mm rifle. We shot at figure-shaped targets from close range to several hundred yards away. Once again, we were being trained to kill, not just shooting at bullseye targets for scores, but at human silhouettes! We were schooled in hand-to-hand combat and even had practice in tossing live hand grenades. (By the way, there was no pulling the pin out with your teeth. You only see that in the movies!)

The kind, gentle, soft-spoken people with whom I had worked in the Colombian campo were being forced into obscurity. And my mental perplexity was becoming a slippery slope – much steeper and harder to traverse than I had imagined. I began to have a change of heart...if I can call it that. In very short order a different kind of apprehension and realization was lowering my resolve and distorting my vision of who I was and where these new circumstances were taking me.

I decided to change at least one aspect of my original, supposedly self-reliant plan.

"I am entering AIT, non? Yes. Then I am dropping my OCS option."

My initial orders were for me to enter AIT (Advanced Individual Training) in Armor at Fort Knox. Initially, naively, I thought when I enlisted that I would work my way "up the ladder," complete all my training requirements, and enter Officer Candidate School. Then, somehow, I'd come out ahead of the pack and once again take charge of my own destiny. I had had a quixotic vision of sparkling stars and bars to say the least. But the rigors and abuse of "Basic" and AIT soon convinced me not to continue pursuing that course. I recognized it was an utterly unachievable fantasy for me.

January 25, 1967

"Whew! Am tired. 5 miles during the day (hiking & marching), 9 - 15 at night. Sleep. The 3rd night, live ammo and land mines; such noise. Smoke, confusion. Flare!. Hit the side of the road. We're home, weary. Foot sore. Whew! Am tired."

I wrote a second letter to Lynne on this same day and, as was often the case, this second one was a poem.

January 25, 1967
The Second of Two Tonight

It's raining for the first time in a
long while
the streets run damp and warm
and cleanse their faces, reflected
on strips of shade where living
things grow tall and slender like
the mulberry bush in a poem that
should be rotund as I remember it
and Monday
and a poem by a stranger to this
face of a small world where we try
to live
and laugh a little whilst the
willow bends and bows forever
and always tho the lite of a new
dawn breaks, bursts over a
mountain where I sit, not alone
but w/ another not strange, nor
unknown but, rather, wanted and
understanding as mortals can do
what we wish tomorrow,
sing, run, fly, walk slowly down a
soft-worn path grown over by
vines
and fallen leaves from last autumn
and the spring before summer
came
we walked in the snow and slipped
and slid and fell and watched and
listened and heard that which was
beautiful to not-deaf ears that
into the sound

that tomorrow bringing much joy
to us and our loved ones as we
love and are happy and sad and
content and share the little hurts
of each day and happiness
promised by the sunshine of
tomorrow, the day after all these
things have come to pass and are
gone, not completely forgotten
what all we had done
but in an instant remember
so, so many wonderful things,
times, friends, things, sounds,
smells, times like snow on
windows
and a song on the radio never
heard by me but others did
and spoke of it
may be strange that this thought
is as long as it seems even tho it <u>is</u>
longer and friends are to
laugh w/ and to cry bitter for a
while
tears and sweet, sweet drops of
glad joy someday soon.

       Sunshine to share…

       I hope that you tan well.

       Love, Denny

We graduated from BCT on **February 4, 1967** and moved right into the next phase of Army training, Advanced Individual Training (AIT). Larry Smith, a confidant, friend, and BCT barracks mate from Chambersburg, PA, and I tried to figure out a way to get his wife, Gloria, and Lynne down for our graduation ceremonies. Unfortunately, our plans did not pan out for a family visit.

In many ways, Armor AIT was a welcome relief from the rigors of intensive physical activity and the relentless mental distress experienced during Basic. Even though AIT was highly structured, it also was much more in line with substantive learning and refining specific skills all of us eventually would use in our military assignments. Another respite was being allowed a bit more leisure during unscheduled evening and weekend hours. These breaks would eventually turn into opportunities for Lynne and me to get together in Louisville or Cincinnati since both cities were reasonably close to the base. Until now, other than Christmas leave, Lynne and I had not seen each other for the past 8+ weeks of Boot Camp.

February 8, 1967

"By the way, AIT is just a bit better than BCT.
1) We have TV in our barracks
2) No classes after 5 pm
3) Saturday afternoon and all Sundays – free"

February 9, 1967

"Got letter from my folks regarding the copyrights to my music."

These were legal papers for registering the copyrights for *Windy Road* and *Two*, the two songs on the 45 RPM record I had recorded October 30, 1966. The record eventually was released while I was in Vietnam.

Ultimately, instead of grueling tedium, I found parts of Armor AIT to be imprudently entertaining. I easily passed my classroom and field tests for radio operation, map reading, and most fun of them all, my driving test to become an officially licensed tank driver. Driving a tank was just plain fun for me; it was almost like driving a very, very, very large go-kart...just a lot slower getting underway, yet with the capability of reaching a top speed of about 40 MPH. (And, of course, with unmitigated firepower.)

"And as I drove down a 60-degree embankment today with 52 tons of steel behind me I thought, 'What is it like to have such power?' Silly boy, we do have it - always have and will - as long as we believe in ... Love."

"Forgot to tell you — on Monday morning I was TC (Tank Commander) at the head of 4 platoons of tanks - a whole company! What a sight! Better believe that DLK stood high in the TC hatch at the front of the formation as we drove through Fort Knox, having traffic stopped for us at all the intersections and — well, there I was, able to stop (or start) 936 tons (1,872,000 pounds—the weight of 16 tanks) of solid steel with the wave of a hand. Such 'poder'." [Spanish word for power]

---0---

For several years after leaving South America I frequently interspersed Spanish words in my writing, and at times in my conversations. I was so accustomed to the bilingual life I had led in South America, where at times I spoke Spanish exclusively over a span of 24 hours or more, that it just flowed naturally.

---0---

Kentucky weather in February 1967 was cold. According to records from weather services, the average nighttime temperature that week in 1967 was 22° F. On those extremely frigid nights, we got up in multiple-hour shifts (mine began at 2:00 am), started and ran the tanks for about a half hour so they wouldn't freeze up. Imagine climbing into a solid steel refrigerator on the coldest winter nights and sitting on a frozen steel seat while you coax, cajole, and pray this beast will come to life and stay running.

I once drove one of our tanks on night maneuvers while completely "buttoned up" -- in total darkness, using only the dimly-lit driver's infrared periscope. (By the way, an infrared image is not "red." The image you actually see is pale green.) As I maneuvered this tracked behemoth on that particular night's exercise, I listened to my TC's intermittent guidance over the closed-circuit tank intercom and visually kept pace with the tiny taillights of the tank in front of me. It took quite a bit of concentration along with coaching from my TC. Meanwhile, all the other tanks in our convoy drove "open hatch" with their drivers' and TCs' heads out. Apparently those TCs did not have the same confidence in their drivers as mine did in me. And, unfortunately, it proved prophetic when one of the inexperienced drivers – even with his hatch open --apparently lost his way, cut a corner too sharply, and slid the tank down a steep embankment onto its side in a dry stream bed. Afterwards, the cadre stood around discussing the training exercise as we cleaned up our "rides." Most had trouble believing that my TC kept us "buttoned up" the entire time... with me in the driver's seat! But my instructor and all our crew knew we had indeed done that! Hooah!

I held onto my official "license" to operate both the M48-A3 and M60-A1 Main Battle "Patton" tanks for many years. I enjoyed pulling it out of my wallet to show people. I have no idea what might have happened to it, but it certainly was uniquely amusing to flash around from time to time and watch people's reactions. Over the years that memento and lots of other memorabilia from my time in the Army and some from my Peace Corps days went missing and are now lost to eternity.

In BCT we received extensive training on the M-14 rifle, the "official" standard issue US Army rifle at that time. The now infamous M-16 was adopted by the Army in 1964 but didn't become standard issue until later due to some major flaws in the design. In Armor AIT we went quite a bit further and received training on additional small arms: the iconic 45 caliber pistol, the 30 caliber Browning Automatic Rifle (BAR for short), the M-79 grenade launcher, and the 45 caliber WWII "grease gun." I remember our instructor telling us, "Ok, gentlemen here's your one chance to play John Wayne. So, go ahead and shoot from the hip if you want." We loaded and fired, repeatedly broke down and cleaned 30 caliber and 50 caliber machine guns, both of which were standard weaponry on the tanks. The latter was a beast to carry on forced hikes. And even though we all took turns sharing this burdensome task, it was brutal. Finally, the main weapon, the 105 mm rifled-barrel cannon, was an utterly deafening monster.

At one point in our training it was rumored that 90% of our company was going to be sent to Vietnam immediately after graduation. The other lucky 10% might make it to Germany where we still had a substantial force stationed. So, while some of the training was interesting and surprisingly enjoyable, it didn't take long for me to realize that I did not want to end up in one of these "steel coffins" in Vietnam. Joyriding along the safe streets of Fort Knox and the unpaved grounds of the training center ultimately could turn into something quite different, even deadly in Vietnam. As that entirely believable rumor made its rounds, its harsh reality struck home...very hard! Once again, I felt an urgent need to find some way of taking control of how I was going to spend my next 2 and one-half years in the Army.

So, late one afternoon, right before "chow time," instead of heading to dinner, I walked to the Personnel Office. Several enlisted men were chatting and taking a smoke break on the porch outside the office. I approached the group and spoke to one of them, a Specialist 5 Gray. (I have no idea what his first name was, nor do I know anything else about him.) I explained my situation and described my Peace Corps service and experience and ultimate "call up." He listened politely and then, responded with a negligible shake of his head – almost a sign of disbelief, then commented softly, "I'll see."

March 8, 1967

"It has been some three days since I last began to write thee. At the moment I am in a sort of "limbo" waiting for my orders to ship out, standing in one place — running away."

Training dragged on but no word or orders came through.

March 19, 1967

"The 19th morning of wind and sun."

"Good morning! It's 2:30 am and I've been on duty for fourteen and a half hours straight. Pués, así es... [Well, that's the way it is.] It's 7:30 am [and] I had thought about writing you every hour last night but, first off, what I wanted to say wouldn't come out because of my exhausted pen, and I was too busy making coffee to try and stay awake and checking the Company area (usually the John). Let me tell you, doll, the kid is dead! Pués, [well] I've only an hour and a half to go - no perspiration and then I'll be able to catch a few Zs."

The weeks continued to drag on interminably. I had lost interest in my classes. Even so, a few odd episodes ensued during this tedium in time.

28 April 1967

"I should be in class but I'm not. Instead, I am sitting in a small room with another man. His face is unshaven, his boots unpolished, his hair unkempt, tangled and uncombed. His fatigues are wrinkled and dirty. He may have had a bath — last week. He stares at his hands and draws a nail clipper to trim a broken nail. He sighs, breathes deeply and looks my way — sad, forlorn. Alas! I fear he is not unlike me tho my appearance is quite different. I am clean-shaven, groomed, & wearing polished boots. Yet, his thoughts must be like mine. Every second he runs farther and farther from this place. Every minute a new step draws him closer to his destination. But it is different; his is a dream — mine is closer to reality. True, I am running with him, not looking back, but he now, is lost; I still tread the crooked, narrow, and treacherous path. I think I shall make it with help. He is trapped — not an animal, but rather, a scared child. It is a sad sight. Together we wait. We shall leave together & go to the same place but for quite different reasons. He there must stay. He is a prisoner & I am his guard. I should be in class, but I'm not. Instead, I'm ..."

"This is one of the most boring things I've done. I even think I'd rather be in class. But, no, I must remain here, guarding this sad, sad man. It is very trying."

—0—

"My roommate [Larry Smith, my buddy from BCT and now AIT] saw his orders yesterday. He's staying in A-7-2 as an instructor. Some of the reserves [National Guard trainees] who are in my class are leaving Sunday. And as of yet, I've heard nothing. Perhaps today."

...and a little later in the same letter...

"It is late, like 9:10 pm. Still, no orders today."

Life seemed to be at an impasse. Then, suddenly -- much to my surprise and even more to my pleasure, new orders for a transfer for me did come through! Within the blink of an eye, I found myself in Personnel School at Fort Knox, learning typing, filing, and all the minutiae of office procedures the US Army embraced at that time. And while the Army normally didn't work this way - especially in terms of transfers, somehow or another good fortune and a sympathetic ear resulted in me moving to a new training center at Fort Knox.

May 5, 1967

I was promoted to E3, PFC (Private First Class), Company A, 7th Battalion, 2nd Training Brigade, Fort Knox, KY.

For the next several months I simply "shuffled" my way along as a clerk of sorts—moving papers from place to place, filing reports, and sometimes delivering mail to other buildings in our complex. Lynne flew into Louisville or Cincinnati to meet me a few times during those months, that is … when I could wrangle a weekend pass.

In order to elicit a degree of empathy (and to be able to register and stay together in a hotel when she visited), we masqueraded as a married couple, including purchasing a small gold band for each of us to wear. We were practically desperate to be with each other whenever we could.

While I was stationed with Company A, my platoon was housed on the bottom floor of a four-story brick barracks. The guys from my platoon were "STRAC," an acronym standing for Strategic, Tough, and Ready Around the Clock. We kept our area and the entrances to the building spotlessly neat. Bunks were always so tightly made that you could actually bounce a twenty-five cent quarter off them (the proverbial test for tight, hospital corners and covers perfectly aligned in every way.) Shoes were always spit-shined, foot lockers perfectly arranged. (Any contraband was secretly stashed above removable panels in the ceiling.)

Conversely, the guys on the floors above, especially the second floor, were much more unkempt and their shoddy housekeeping led to our CO (Commanding Officer) restricting the entire building to base on a particular weekend.

Unfortunately, this was a weekend Lynne had already booked a flight to Kentucky. So, I approached our Barracks Sergeant and pleaded my case. The sergeant firmly stated he could not countermand the CO's orders. Then, with a furtive wink, he quietly said, "You know, what the Army don't know ain't gonna hurt 'em." And in an even softer voice he said, "There's a garbage truck leaving base at 0500 with an empty passenger seat. Be back on base before roll call Monday and ... be careful."

Lynne and I had a wonderful weekend sequestered in the Tijuana Motel in Muldraugh, KY....and Lynne still has the receipt from that stealthy, covert rendezvous in her scrapbook.

June 5, 1967

I wrote to Lynne about other peculiar, albeit amusing, goings-on in the Company C Mess Hall.

"Seems that someone perpetually is changing the letters on the menu board that should say 'Welcome to Company C Mess Hall' to ... 'Welcome to Company C Mass Hell'..." [and other unusual and creative phrases].

But even more surprising was this observation... *"Festooned on the wall of the dining room is a large painting of vines and flowers woven about and around a Jewish Thanksgiving, Protestant Grace, and Catholic Prayer....and intertwined with the delicate green vines are the letters F T A written in beautiful script. Truly a masterpiece! So now we have an ornate wall, decorated with appropriate inscriptions (fitting no less) and the symbols for insurgence within the ranks that are no less than well-known throughout Army installations world over ...FTA ... Fuck The Army ..."*

Some "I could care less" career NCOs often joked that this stood for "Fun Travel and Adventure." But we all knew better.

A week or so later I requested and was granted several days' leave to attend a special event in my hometown of York, PA. One of my original music compositions, *Through My Window,* was being performed by a chorus at the Central York High School graduation ceremonies (my old high school) and I was invited to attend as a special guest. Later that week I took the 10-hour bus ride from Fort Knox to York to attend the graduation ceremonies.

I mentioned in the author's note at the outset of this book my love of music began very early in life. The pre-WWII, 1940s Big Band Sounds are indelibly etched into my subconscious. I have watched "The Glenn Miller Story" innumerable times, indeed, too many to count. In the movie there is an amusing and peculiarly analogous scene to what occurred to me at this graduation.

In the movie Glenn (played by Jimmy Stewart) and his wife, Helen (played by June Allyson), are sitting in a club, listening to the first public performance of his signature ballad, *Moonlight Serenade.* Unfortunately, the specific band arrangement (changed by the club's band leader) was nothing like what Glenn intended the song to be. He turned to his wife and said, "I wrote this as a ballad; this guy turned it into a hootchie-cootchie."

Now, as I listened to the young voices of the chorus performing my song, I was almost as taken aback as Glenn appeared to be in the movie. Instead of the wistful, reflective ballad I had written, the high school band conductor had rearranged my composition into something more appropriate for a marching band! Lynne told me later that she couldn't even look at me during the performance because she didn't want to see the expression on my face. She knew I would be just as flabbergasted as she was.

Regardless of the presentation, it was still an honor to have my music performed, and Lynne and I spent some wonderful, albeit all-too-short hours together before I had to return to base.

June 15, 1967

"Tis très sad to be apart when the seedling has only but begun to sprout & needs ever-so-much more attention & care. But perhaps this will allow us to see if that new life be strong or weak; if it shall fare gamely or shudder, weaken, and fall."

June 15, 1967 (a separate letter written the same day)

"The forever blue nite, a few shimmers of lite above, the gentle chirp of crickets, a dampening lawn spattered with the tan of sun-toasted blades of grass, the deep shadow of sleeping trees, loneliness, wanting you dear, dear Lynne. There is a lone street lite not far from where I sit. In a way I am like it, quiet now but glowing because I have found happiness & love. In a way, too, I am different. Tomorrow the soft glimmer will fade w/ the early lite of dawn but I will continue to radiate because I love."

June 17, 1967

By now I had professed my desire and affection in innumerable ways, but Lynne and I both knew that while we felt an incredible mutual attraction, a longer, more binding commitment would be something we would need to consider ever so much more carefully. Lynne was still reeling after withdrawing from a difficult and nasty relationship while I was floundering in not knowing where I was going or what I eventually would do with my life.

Again, I turned to reflections of much more serene, comforting, and pleasant memories.

"<u>I want you</u>! Because you are Lynne — tiny, sweet, warm, cuddly, tender — yet strong, soft, lovely, divine, fun, gentle, & precious to me."

"Because of things we've done—Nov 9, letters, phone calls, Christmas, New Year's Eve, songs, friends, drinks, pizza, Muldraugh, L/ville, Cinci, letters to friends, zoo, movies, 60 second shops, museum, Chinese restaurants, Pepsi and beer on rugs, sport coats, foam, Washington, VW, Philadelphia, Fayetteville, Gettysburg, Summit (& thereabouts) the PA Pike, the NJ Pike, H Johnson's, vegetable soup and Sprite, cheese & tuna, stroganoff, Washington House, Hawks, P/ville Pool, Speelgrund, West Chester, country roads, shooting, riding the tractor in the snow, walking in the snowy woods, grasshoppers, non-flambé, spaghetti, noises, and ----, music, The Emerald Suite, Uncle Gene's Office, Chris and Gene's home, snake in a baby carriage, soccer, Ev Dirksen, I want you, contract, 5 cent bet (& I'm going to win!), peonies, cats, mattresses, touching, & so, so much more, & beginning to love, being happy & content together, together....."

By the end of June, I had moved into a new personnel position. I was now assigned to Company C, Special Troops, Office of the Adjutant General, Fort Knox, KY, and working in the *Enlisted Overseas Levy Division*. Suddenly I was now the person in charge of processing and posting who was being transferred somewhere — could be anywhere across the globe — both new AIT graduates as well as currently assigned higher ranking enlisted personnel. I seemed to have regained a modicum of control over my life....at least it appeared that on the surface. But I worked at this new position almost as an automaton. It didn't matter to me who these men and women were or where they were being posted. I didn't know them; I didn't recognize any of their names; I knew absolutely nothing about them. I just had to fill empty slots with a qualified (on paper) body. I really wasn't in control of anything, including my own destiny -- as I was about to find out.

June 28, 1967

"It is very early. We began at 4:45 am. The CO (ass that he is) decided we should have a shakedown ... they found a bottle of aspirin and 2 NoDoze tablets."

"The new job is going fairly well but — wow! is there a bunch of work! We got a levy for Nam from DA (Department of the Army) yesterday afternoon. For four hours I broke down that mess into Command, MOS [Military Occupational Specialty] & Grade.....needless to say O/S Assignments is so much better than M&D."

"My new office phones are 4-5711, 4-6956, and 4-7342.....we are constantly utilizing all three lines — mainly to Department of the Army, OPO in Washington, DC."

July 9, 1967

"I've been working long and arduous hours. Friday I worked from 7 am until 11 pm. Saturday 8 - 5:30 and now it's Sunday 1 pm and I'm almost caught up."

"Off the Record" Requests and "On the Record, Off I Go"

There were times during my tenure at the Overseas Levy Desk when a senior officer would come to me and covertly ask me to "86" the transfer of a specific soldier scheduled to be deployed overseas. (This person was usually an aide to the officer or to the officer's immediate superior.) I did this surreptitiously -- "under the table"— simply by changing the Eligibility Code on a computer index "punch" card and moving it to a deferred file or "unavailable for service." This was a very simple process.

However, when my name popped up for deployment to Vietnam, that ploy didn't work. My Commanding Officer would not let me change my own classification or my destination. There was even another clerk in our office who stepped up and volunteered to go to Vietnam in my place. But the CO steadfastly refused to let this happen.

My orders from Army HQ in Washington indicated I was to be assigned to Headquarters and Headquarters Detachment (HHD), 43rd Signal Battalion, 1st Signal Brigade, Pleiku, Vietnam. I really had no idea where that was or what I was about to get into halfway around the world in the increasingly controversial war being waged there. The orders for my deployment stated I was to report for deployment to "USAOSREPLSTA Fort Lewis, Washington by 12 December 1967."

Chapter Three

"Where Have All the Flowers Gone?"
Kingston Trio; Peter, Paul & Mary
(Written by Pete Seeger -1955)

July 24, 1967

"'To where now?' he asked his soul. 'Onward. Onward and upward even higher,' was the reply. Then this we shall do."

Lynne and I had chatted informally and talked in a tentative way about the idea of our getting married ... sometime ... maybe ... perhaps? Obviously, extenuating circumstances would complicate whatever we chose to do. How would my pending deployment change things? We had teased each other and fantasized about the possibility of a Spring wedding...maybe the following May; but again, nothing concrete. Should we?

Lynne and I both were apprehensive and unsure what direction our lives might or should or possibly *could* take. I was leaving the country for a war zone in December. Would our young, budding, delicate relationship stand up during a year, our very first one, separated by 9,000 miles? Would it or could it survive the inherent trials and tribulations, worries and fear of such a separation? Could there possibly be any advantages to our getting married before I left? How about disadvantages? And, what about the worst possible scenario that we completely avoided, daring not to mention, let alone ... discuss?

A few friends and even some of our family members cautioned us about being hasty in our decision to get married. But in the end, Lynne and I decided to trust love — our very new, very young love — over all else. We planned our wedding for late November, several months away and just a few weeks before my flight left for Vietnam.

---0---

August 25, 1967

Lynne's birthday was coming up soon (August 29). Concluding that money couldn't buy what I wanted to give her – happiness and contentment forever -- I couldn't come up with anything to buy her for a birthday present. Instead, I composed the following song as a special gift.

"Lynne's Song"

I want to walk in the sand on a misty day
Down by the sea where the gulls soar and children play,
Down with the waves where they tumble and curl
In on the beach with a warm, foamy swirl.
I want to walk on a silvery white shore
And I'll not pause a moment but forever more.

I want to stroll in the rain and the gentle breeze
Down by the bay that flows out to the roaming seas
I want to wander for hours on end
I want to share all these joys with a friend.
I want to amble 'neath blue skies above
And I'll pass all these moments with Lynne whom I love.

God grant me moments to spend near the ocean's side.
God grant me love that flows on like the thundering tide.
God grant me wisdom and courage to live.
Grant me humility so I can give
All of my life to the one I adore
And we'll walk on together, forever more.

For the next few weeks my letters became fewer and more scattered in thought, but I continued to write musings of love and poetry, rhymes, and unmitigated statements of my devotion. We anxiously waited for these last, stressful days to pass.

August 31, 1967

I was promoted to Specialist E-4.

October 18, 1967

"A story I thee shall tell."

"I suppose I'm getting to be an old man. An old man in love with Lynne. [but] for a while tonight I thought that I was still a young fellow. And, indeed I am still—at heart."

"This eve' I sauntered outside in the brisk autumn air. Twas' really chilly — just about right for a November football game. Now I'm back inside ... and I am still ... and sore."

"We played tackle football (without equipment) for about an hour and a half. Luckily, I'm only a bit weary. J.R. [Hodge] has a bruised ankle. Searcy has a twisted ankle and bad knee. Guye has a pulled calf muscle and a few of the other youngsters have a few bumps and bruises."

Ah…the invincibility and ignorance of youth….and not the last of the bumps, bruises, and breaks a number of us would receive during the ensuing year.

Our Wedding Day Arrives

November 25, 1967

Our wedding was scheduled for 7:00 pm at Saint John's Episcopal Church in York, PA. A light rain was falling as Lynne and I drove to the church in separate vehicles; both of us wondered, "Is the rain an omen?"

Lynne was the first of our wedding party to arrive at the church. And a bit of panic set in almost immediately — there were no flowers to be found anywhere! Lynne had ordered them. She had been assured they would be delivered on time and she had even sent me the confirmation information. Turns out, there had been an afternoon wedding there that same day and in the haste to clean up in preparation for our ceremony, all of the flowers in the church -- including the unopened boxes containing our bride's bouquet, the attendants' bouquets, the garlands for the pews, and the men's boutonnières were thrown into the church dumpster!

Two of my groomsmen, friends from Fort Knox, Larry Smith and John Hodge quickly retrieved them from the dumpster. Fortunately, they were intact since the flowers were still unwrapped in their original boxes. But, what a way to start!

The wedding began at 7:00 pm, moved right along at a decent pace … but wait! Another little glitch arose. There were no prayer books or guides up front for the wedding party. But, since the Episcopal ceremony and the Catholic ceremony were reasonably similar … and being the good Catholic that he was … John had it all memorized and conveniently guided us along, whispering instructions in advance of what to do or say.

At last, Lynne and I walked down the aisle happily married … with tears in our eyes.

I could blame my tears on happiness, and in fact, for the most part they were. I was simply overcome with pure joy. But, one more time on this special day, something else was amiss. As we got into the car and started the short drive to visit Lynne's Grandma Horne (who was too frail to attend the ceremony) I had trouble breathing. Apparently, I was allergic to Lynne's flowers! We stopped the car and stuffed the flowers in the trunk…and the rest of the evening was filled with undeniable joy, music, food, and celebration. In fact, the party continued long after Lynne and I departed for our honeymoon in Cape May, NJ. Sans us, friends and family celebrated this special day by rolling up the Persian carpets in the Warfield's living room and dancing the night away.

Chapter Four

"Leaving on a Jet Plane"
John Denver; Peter, Paul & Mary
(Written by John Denver - 1966)

My orders stated I was to report *"NLT 1200 12 Dec 67 to USAOSREPLSTA, Ft Lewis Wash 98433. Security clearance: Secret."* They went on to list immunizations needed including one for *"Plague"* (at the top of the list), what to wear (summer khakis and short-sleeved shirt), and a few other things we were allowed to bring. One sentence stands out in an amusing, yet oxymoronic way. *"The introduction, purchase and possession of privately owned weapons is prohibited in RVN."*

Wait a minute…..aren't we going to a war zone where people have lots of guns….little ones, middle-size ones, big ones, boom-Boom-BOOM ones? Oh well, pretty sure they'll give me something when I get there.

Since I had been the clerk in charge of overseas deployments at Fort Knox, I was able to wrangle a flight from the US to Vietnam for myself and for my good friend, John Hodge, whose levy for Vietnam had come up the same time as mine. John worked as an accountant in the same office at Fort Knox as I did. We lived in the same barracks and we became close friends. In fact, as mentioned in the previous chapter, he was one of my groomsmen. He drove straight through, all the way from Cleveland to be in our wedding party. I scheduled our flights so that we would celebrate the holidays early, leave just before Christmas 1967, and then, at least theoretically, be back home in time for Christmas when we returned from our deployments in 1968.

Second week of December 1967

It's not easy to describe the pain of leaving Lynne. Our extended hugs, not wanting to let go of each other and our last tear-streamed moments are a sad image ingrained in my memory, a memory that can never ever be erased.

Thursday, December 14, 1967 1:40 am – waiting, waiting

"I am in the desert, barren alone, empty, parched, dry and ungraced. How grotesque! Yet I can blossom. With the gift of a tear from the sky my limbs can sprout and flourish."

"Man for long did not know this — he has learned — after years. Lucky us — we have less than that to bear."

3:00 pm Pacific Time 15 (Friday)

"We've been airborne for 8 hours. Originally, we were to have left at 10:10 pm last night but that was pushed back to 3:10 am and finally at 7:05 am we left. All this time there was no place to sleep — so a bit tired are we at the moment."

"I met John in Cleveland without difficulty as you know, since I phoned [later] from Chicago. We got to Seattle-Tacoma on schedule and decided not to report until morning. (We stayed in a motel near the airport.) On Tuesday morning we caught a bus at 7:00 am which took us to Fort Lewis. After processing in, we were assigned a day of details and, as per usual, John and I pulled KP together. It seems to never fail. Yesterday then, we finished processing out - turning in linens, etc. and caught our flight early this morning."

Pulling KP together with John was not exactly by chance, as I might have made it sound. When it came to temporary duty, which everyone pulled from time to time, John had hatched a strategy that we had implemented back at Fort Knox. The plan meant going against a timeless unwritten rule of Army volunteerism, "Never volunteer for anything!" Yet, together we did the unthinkable. We both volunteered for KP, the proverbial kitchen drudgery that is often administered as light punishment. But we didn't just sit and peel potatoes interminably. You see, not only did we volunteer for KP, we volunteered for scrubbing pots and pans! John's thought (and it turned out to be right on point) was that there usually were no pots to clean at the outset of KP since they were all being used to prepare the meal. And once they had been used, they generally needed to be cleaned only once before the next chow service when another crew would take over. Whereas washing dishes and bussing tables was a constant, on-the-go throughout the meal exhausting duty, pots and pans was a relatively brief workload. Until they needed to be cleaned, John and I sat outside the kitchen area and "had a smoke" with some of the cooks. And at the end of our scrubbing stint, voilà ... we were done and off we went! Interesting and reasonably sensible solution I would never have thought of testing.

"I doubt if you can imagine how more reassuring it is (wrong phrase but —) to have come this far with John. These last few days we've sort of helped each other along, trying to be funny at times, speaking seriously at others."

"Fort Lewis is total confusion. 15% AWOL no one knowing where anyone is "<u>at</u>." If I had to go through it again, I think I'd blow my mind. It's really very bad."

"After we reach Japan (our one stop) there'll be a short (I hope) layover, then off to Cam Ranh Bay. From there — who knows? As either JR or I mentioned, there is no telling where one will be sent. John (sitting beside me, reading a war

story about the Navy!) said he wants to include a few lines so I'll let him stick in his part here and continue shortly thereafter."

(In John's handwriting below mine.)

*"Love you —
Want you —
Need you —
Miss you —
Love — "*

9:00 pm Friday the 15th (PA time)

"We've just taken off from Asato Airbase Okinawa headed for Yakota Airbase. There are two stops; the first for fuel, the second for a change of crew. I'm really confused by this change in time (zones) but I imagine I'll get used to it."

Tuesday December 19, 1967

"Hi honey! Welcome to Cam Ranh Bay. John and I arrived safely Saturday at 8:00 pm. At present we are at the 22nd Replacement Battalion, Cam Ranh Bay. As I mentioned before - we know not whither we goest*. We should know within a day or two." [*"Wither Thou Goest" was one of many songs performed at our wedding.]

The airbase at Cam Ranh Bay was located about halfway up the east coast of South Vietnam. It was an enormous complex consisting of one area designated as a deep-water port, another land area with several long 10,000+ foot runways directly adjacent to the South China Sea, another area set aside for a US Army Convalescent Center on a sandy beach north of the airstrip, plus areas designated for Assigned Duty Personnel barracks and Transient Personnel barracks.

Physically, the bay itself was about 16 miles long, the military base (land area) surrounding it nearly 20 miles long and 10 miles across. This enormous logistics aggregate was capable of handling the transfer of personnel, equipment, materials, and supplies of any sort needed throughout this nearly 20-year war. The airfield was engineered to allow the largest possible aircraft in existence at that time to land and take off. It was shared by multiple US military services: Army, Navy, Marine Corps, and Air Force. Each service had its own general area of operations, but all shared the long airstrip and the deep-water port as needed.

As for the Convalescent Center, all injured or wounded soldiers in II Corps received initial treatment from a medic in their unit. If more advanced treatment was needed, they were transported to an Evacuation Hospital, many times by Med Evac or "Dust Off" helicopter. Following completion of their treatment, they were returned to their units. Ambulatory patients requiring additional (30 days or less) rehab were sent to the US Army 6th Convalescent Center (6th CC) at Cam Ranh Bay. Finally, any soldiers who required more advanced treatment for their wounds or injuries or for any illness from tropical diseases were airlifted by Military Transport to hospitals in Japan or the continental United States.

While certainly nicer than a field hospital, 6th CC was not exactly a luxury convalescent center, although it was located right next to a sandy beach available for use by the patients. The facility housed 1300 beds, about 750-850 filled with patients at any given time, all of whom were attended by 8 doctors. The wards at 6th CC were rather rustic, built exactly the same as typical wooden US Army barracks.

The Convalescent Center was not too far from the Transient Barracks where John and I stayed. These were bare-bones wooden structures. Interior walls were unfinished. A row of steel frame, single cot or bunk beds stretched along the length of each side of a single, center aisle. Interior lighting for the barracks was also minimalist -- bare bulbs dangling from exposed, although insulated, rough wiring stapled across or hung between the ceiling rafters.

I don't remember much from our two or three days at Cam Ranh Bay other than a lot of waiting around, sand, heat, and boredom. There was a Post Exchange (PX) and NCO Club. The latter is where John and I ran into Charlie Webb, a guy we both knew from Fort Knox. Charlie had been wounded during his tour and was recovering at the Convalescent Center. He was full of stories, including one about a Drill Sergeant we all had at Fort Knox. Seems that hard-nosed Drill Sergeant had been wounded by "friendly fire" and the question was whether it was deliberate or not -- as a payback for the tough time he gave many of our fellow troops at Knox. (He had been shot in a most sensitive area and apparently was unable to sit.)

One of the first things Charlie offered us was a "toke" (marijuana), something I had never tried before. I took a puff or two and immediately regretted it. I had a reaction that made me lose my voice. I simply could not utter a word. I swore off it immediately and never touched it again.

Wednesday, December 20, 1967

"Dearest Lynne, Just a note to tell you how very, very much I love you. John and I have, together sworn that neither shall drink excessively, nor smoke pot, nor be unfaithful for the next year."

"John and I went to Mass the day after we arrived — I was with <u>thee</u> there."

"Together We Walk Day by Day."

This last line in the letter was a lyric from another song I wrote for Lynne while at Fort Knox. Although Lynne is a classically trained pianist, she and I sang this as a duet many times over the years.

Charlie went home shortly after we saw him. Sometime later, Lynne mailed him a copy of my record, *"Windy Road"* as soon as it was released. Charlie had heard me sing at a bar we frequented near Fort Knox as well as on base in some informal jams with other GIs. My favorite memory of one these took place while on a break during a long hike during BCT. Our DI had heard several of us singing some "doo wop" in the barracks. So, as we waited for trucks to pick us up and haul us back to barracks, the DI insisted that I gather some of "my backup singers" and perform an a cappella version of "In the Still of the Night" We did, and had fun doing it. It was a welcome relief for the guys who had been humping those heavy backpacks in the heat.

A day or two later, John and I finally received specific orders for our final assignments in Vietnam. John was assigned to the 17th Aviation Group at Nha Trang, just up the coast, only 30 miles north of Cam Ranh Bay. I was assigned to the 43rd Signal Battalion in Pleiku in the middle of the Central Highlands – the same unit as stated in my original orders. Those orders indicated, "Pleiku," yet I still wasn't sure precisely where that city was located. I hadn't bothered to look it up on a map before I left. Even if I had, we were told that our assignments would likely be changed as soon as we arrived in country anyway due to DEROSs (Date of Estimated Return from Overseas Service) and WIA or KIA immediate replacement needs. So, there was no guarantee any of us would end up where our original orders had stated.

In 1967, Pleiku covered an area of a little over 102 square miles – about the size of Orlando, FL, despite being much less densely populated. The area covered by the Central Highlands all-told was about 20,000 square miles – roughly the size of West Virginia. Camp Holloway also had been mentioned as a possible post for me, and that raised some concern since it was the site of several previous, vicious enemy attacks. Regardless of my ignorance upon my arrival, my knowledge of Vietnam geography would expand significantly in the coming year.

Chapter Five

"500 Miles"
The Journeymen; Kingston Trio; Peter, Paul, & Mary
(Written by Hedy West - 1961)

The skies were overcast, but not threatening when a driver picked me up in a nondescript, aka typical, open-sided, canvas-top jeep. The US Army "Spec 4" driver and I had little to no conversation during the ten-minute trip from the 22nd Replacement Center at Cam Ranh Bay to *Dong Ba Thin* Base Camp. The camp was situated on the narrow, landside neck of Cam Ranh Bay, almost directly across the water from the 6th Convalescent Center. The camp was home to the 5th Special Forces Group and MACV-SOG Operations during the war. It had its own short asphalt airstrip, *Dong Ba Thin Airfield* and also a highly active, albeit small, *Flanders Army Heliport*. My Vietnam adventure truly was about to get off to a marvelous "flying" start.

I shouted a brief "Thanks!" to the driver above the din of the engine and whistling sound of spinning blades of a UH-1 "Huey" helicopter preparing for lift-off right next to the Dispatcher's post. Then, in a surprisingly swift manner, I was directed to board that same Huey. I say "swift manner" because my jeep had barely pulled in, I flashed my orders to the dispatcher who briefly eyeballed them, whereupon he immediately told me to climb on board that noisy chopper on the dirt and grass landing zone.

As blades of the chopper continued "spooling up," I did the proverbial, semi-crouch, duck-down walk as I crossed a narrow strip of steel PSP (Perforated Steel Planking) used for runways and sometimes for walkways. The shrill whining of the engine and unmistakable whir of the spinning blades were earsplitting. It was so loud and difficult to hear that the crew chief -- door gunner simply motioned for me to sit in the canvas sling chair directly in front of him, behind the pilot and right next to the open door on the starboard (right) side. I clicked the buckle of my lap belt and literally sucked in my breath, holding it briefly as we lifted off and hovered just a few feet above the ground. It was an exhilarating sensation! I loved it from the start—and I enjoyed every one of the dozens of trips I took in those amazing machines, even some much more harrowing rides later in my year-long tour. Compared to the time prior to and immediately after my arrival in country, things were beginning to move very swiftly.

We hung there for a few seconds and I hastily scanned the individuals and small groups of GIs standing nearby. Some were sitting on rucksacks, many appeared bored from waiting, and many had a vacant stare or the look of apprehension on their faces.

...and we were off, pivoting slightly and pitching forward a few degrees, the unmistakable blade slap beginning to echo across the landscape beneath us. We climbed quickly as our flight path took us out over the South China Sea before we turned northwest, darting over the thick, green, tropical landscape towards Pleiku.

Electrifying is probably the best word to describe that first chopper ride with doors wide open, wind whistling as it swirled into and rushed by the cabin. Even today as I write this, I have truly vivid mental images and positive, almost euphoric feelings from the moment I climbed aboard and throughout my first ride in that Huey.

We landed at Camp Holloway, the US Army helicopter base about 3 miles east of Pleiku city. I hopped off and began to walk away, shaking my head slowly from side to side. It was a sign of my awe and near disbelief. I repeatedly glanced back over my shoulder at this incredible machine, the rotors still spinning as the pilot prepared to take off again. This extraordinary machine had just whisked me rather magically across rice paddies and rolling hills to the densely forested mountains of Vietnam. I paused one last moment and the pilot gave me a thumbs up for good luck - which I returned. Then I smiled broadly and waved to him again, not knowing what might lie ahead for either of us.

I checked in at the Camp Holloway dispatch office and they phoned the 43rd to request transportation. Soon after, a jeep from the 43rd arrived to pick me up. I was now "in-country" and perhaps just as noteworthy, passably naive about what to expect in this new segment of my rather unorthodox jigsaw puzzle of life.

December 23, 1967

"Dearest Darling Lynne,"

"How do I love thee? Ne'er could I count all the ways — there are too too many. John and I have parted paths for the moment — more later."

"I'm at Headquarters, 43rd Sig as planned - but altho we're close, we're not in Camp Holloway."

Lynne had waited anxiously for this first letter written by me from Vietnam. After nearly three agonizing weeks, it finally arrived. In it, I told her I had arrived safely and I gave her the APO address where she could begin sending mail to me.

And to me from Lynne, coincidentally written on that very same day:

Saturday, The 23rd December

Dear, dear Denny –

And then one day it happened – the postman brought a letter. But you know what? The letter was marked "3" and it is my first!

Tho it has not yet been two weeks, I longed so much for a letter. And now one has come and I am so happy. And also today – the box mailed in Seattle Dec 12 that took all of 12 days to cross the country--and your letter came halfway across the world in 2 days!

And, thus our international, multiple time zones, sometimes perplexing and often disjointed correspondence began. Not surprisingly, my wife had not been idle during those first anxious days.

Wednesday, December 27, 1967

Darling—An address at last! From your letter: 'You should be able to write a book by now, not having written since I left.'

But – Dear Denny – you were wrong I have been writing ever since you left. And here they come …17 letters in all. I love you.

Indeed, we both had been writing but not necessarily mailing our letters during those first, emotionally exhausting and anxiety-ridden days.

During the course of the ensuing year we both found time to write, some weeks nearly every day, periodically more than once a day, still others with gaps of days between notes. Without fail, correspondence between us was inconsistent to say the least. According to the postmark and the handwritten and (sometimes) initialed date of arrival in country, letters, packages, and audiotapes were dependent on the availability of space on transport as well as subject to the whims of Mother Nature. At one point during my tour in Southeast Asia, I wrote that mail to our unit had been held up for what seemed an interminable amount of time -- nearly three weeks due to the Monsoons and weather-related issues in the South China Sea. So, while I might be writing in response to something Lynne had written in a previous note, she might be doing the same…and our letters would cross in the mail…and sometimes be delivered out of order and end up totally confusing to say the least.

As welcoming and comforting as it was to receive mail of any sort, my initial days spent traveling thousands of miles and crossing the International Date Line, arriving in country and finally arriving at my duty station were filled mostly with simple rudimentary work details.

And, while I still had no idea what ultimately would be in store for me, my anxious moments apparently bore no resemblance to the hand-wringing hours my wife and family, as well as thousands of other families like ours, were spending. No news (of a personal nature) was not necessarily good news for them. Those empty days often increased their concern and apprehension, especially when the only "up-to-the-minute" news they were able to get was what they saw on television. In 1967-68 there was no Facebook or email, no Skype or Facetime. In fact, Lynne and I did not physically "see" each other or "talk" to each other for the next 9 months (until we met for R&R in Hawaii). We did exchange audiotapes, which meant we could hear each other's voices, but the inability to actually talk to each other and respond in real time was undeniably stressful to say the least.

Chapter Six

"A Hundred Pounds of Clay"
Gene McDaniels
(Written by Kay Rogers, Luther Dixon, & Bob Elgin - 1967)

Finally! Two days before Christmas 1967 I arrived at my official duty station, Headquarters and Headquarters Detachment (HHD) 43rd Signal Battalion, 21st Signal Group, 1st Signal Brigade, Pleiku.

We were under the command of the 1st Signal Brigade, the unit in charge of providing communications throughout all of South Vietnam from coast to jungle and throughout the mountain areas. This widespread and geographically diverse area required a broad variety of signal resources to cover it effectively. Those resources included land line telephones, teletype, radio relay, microwave, photographic services, cryptographic coding, and satellite communications, as well as courier service. The Vietnam War was the first-ever use of satellite communications in a combat zone. Some of our equipment was located in the 43rd Battalion A Company compound immediately next to us on what was nicknamed "Tropo Hill." HHD and A Company compounds were separated by a simple, interwoven, hinge-joint barbed wire fence about six feet high. This was similar to 8x8 wire livestock-style fencing, except that every strand, both vertical and horizontal, was made of barbed wire.

Tropo Hill compound hosted a variety of communications gear including several giant antennas (4, 120-foot-high and 6, 60-foot-high screens), all facing slightly different directions — for both sending and/or receiving signals. Apparently, some signals from these giant screens were "bounced" off the troposphere. I never understood the technology, but that wasn't part of my job - so no big deal. It wasn't part of my job to explain; it was, in the vernacular, "above my pay grade."

I assumed I would be working in my assigned MOS as a "Personnel Specialist" (a generic, albeit fancy title for a records clerk). In other words, I would be an office worker responsible for typing up orders and reports, requisitions and the like, along with filing virtual reams of all those things, many of the things I had done at Fort Knox.

But upon arrival and even before I was assigned a desk of my own, I was given "fatigue duty," temporary day duty -- as every enlisted man was at one time or another -- filling sandbags. These gray woven cloth bags were filled with about 40 pounds of sand each and were used to reinforce the revetments – barriers that measured about two-feet wide by several feet high. These low sandbag walls, stacked near or against the sides of buildings, provided protection from shrapnel and flying debris – but not a direct hit. Some "blast walls" housing A Company personnel on Tropo Hill directly adjacent to us were built with a slightly modified design. The walls in those consisted of 55-gallon drums filled with sand or dirt placed every two feet and interspaced with stacks of sandbags between them. Sandbags were used to build the machine gun bunker at the entrance to our compound where a pair of sentries monitored individuals and vehicles approaching 24 hours a day, every day. Sandbags also were used to construct defensive bunkers on our perimeter.

Two interesting things took place during the hot, dull, grimy, and drudgery-filled hours of my first days. At one point our sandbagging group of about a dozen men, mostly very, very young inductees, was asked, "Does anyone here know how to drive a Deuce and a Half (2½-ton truck)?" No hands went up; these were all naïve, young cherries and FNGs (Fucking New Guys) like me, albeit most were a bit younger than me.

Thinking that this possibly could get me out of tiresome, repetitive, dirty, and sweat-filled hours of shoveling, filling and tying bags, I raised my hand…even though I had never sat inside, let alone driven a Deuce and a Half in my life. "After all," I thought to myself, "how hard could it be?" I had grown up driving my dad's tractors and stick-shift cars from the time I was 11 years old. Plus, within the past year I had been trained and licensed by the US Army to drive a 52-ton Patton tank!

Another GI was assigned to ride "shotgun" and accompany me on our trek. We both picked up rifles, helmets and flak vests from the armory, then walked to the motor pool on the opposite side of the compound. Once there, we signed out a truck and began our trip to the sand pit where a bulldozer and wheeled front-loader were waiting to fill the back of our truck with several tons of sand.

So here I was, new in country — a war zone no less — and me exhibiting a bit of the somewhat misguided, perhaps foolish bravado I had developed living alone (at 18 years of age) and doing all kinds of fascinating things during my Peace Corps stint in South America just a short year and a half before. Of course, in South America I never drove a motorized vehicle since my main mode of transportation during my first year was on horseback or on foot. Then it was buses and taxis that transported me around Bogotá during my second year. Now, here I was, about to drive a 10-wheel truck -- figuratively "flying by the seat of my pants" halfway around the world. What a change!

We got verbal directions to the quarry, operated by the 20th Engineer Battalion somewhere off of Highway 14. The engineer compound was north-northeast of our compound and the quarry was somewhere between them, Artillery Hill -- not far from Lake Biển Hồ, a picturesque but unsecure area known to be a favorite Viet Cong hideout peppered with tunnels and concealed safe havens. The trip was supposed to be a relatively short one, just a few miles, so we wanted to be careful not to make any wrong turns. As we climbed into the truck and began to drive toward the quarry, I had no reservations about getting to the quarry and back. But I did have one mildly troubling thought. I hoped I wouldn't have to back up the truck.

Patterns for shifting are relatively similar on many stick-shift vehicles. Would they be the same on this truck? There were no markings on the knob of the gearshift sticking up through the floor directly over the transmission. Where was the reverse slot? I knew how to double clutch and shift gears forward but had no idea how to back this big rig up. I mentally crossed my fingers as we pulled in behind several other trucks waiting to be filled. As I eased the truck forward I kept whispering to myself, "Get it right, get it right ... pull straight into the center of the drop area ... don't make me back up!" ... and ... Phew! I managed somehow to ease it into position just under the loader without having to put it in reverse. What a relief!

Loaded with several tons of sand, we motored back and parked near the north perimeter at the 43rd compound, leaving our payload to be shoveled off by the next day's sandbag detail.

Little did I know that the next day would provide the second significant change in my Army "assignments," the first being my fortuitous transfer out of Armor School and into Personnel School at Fort Knox.

Once again, I found myself assigned to fatigue duty between the barracks area and the north perimeter of our compound. I was helping shovel sand off the truck I had driven the day before. A GI by the name of SP4 James Lindstrom walked up to our detail and asked, "Does anyone here know how to write?" At first, I thought it was an odd question. Didn't these guys all have to know how to write to get into the Army? Or, was the Army so desperate these days that they would induct illiterates? (In truth, the latter was on the brink of the Army's desperate reality.) Lindstrom continued, "We're looking for someone who knows how to write news releases and stories. Anybody here able to do that?"

Apparently, Lindstrom's DEROS was within a month. In short, he was going home and was looking for someone to replace him as the unit Information Specialist, Journalist, and Assistant Editor of the monthly Unit Newsletter, *The Unicorn*. Once again, I went against the time-honored admonition about *not* volunteering for anything in the Army. Without hesitating, I raised my hand and spoke up. I figured this potentially could be a much more interesting job than sitting in an office pushing papers and being a file clerk REMF (Rear Echelon Mother Fucker). REMFs were what most troops behind the lines, away from most of the fighting, were called by troops engaged directly with the enemy at the front.

Eventually, as the US found out, "the front" was not as easily defined as it had been in previous wars. In Vietnam it ended up being virtually everywhere – from dense, critter-infested, impossible to see more than 3 yards in front of you jungle and Mekong Delta swamp to city streets and alleys, to hardwood mountain forests with tangled, interwoven, virtually impenetrable triple-canopy that hid much of the Ho Chi Minh Trail.

The trail was an elaborate series of footpaths, jungle and mountain trails, roads, and bridges begun in 1959. It snaked its way from just south of Hanoi through parts of neighboring Laos and eastern Cambodia, continuing along nearly the entire length of Vietnam. Offshoots from the main trail turned east and edged towards the interior of South Vietnam. It apparently ended just west of Dalat, less than 200 miles from Saigon. It was the Communists' major supply route between North and South Vietnam and was so complex and sophisticated that portions of it were actually paved in the 1960s to allow truck traffic.

In his best Walter Cronkite voice Lindstrom advised me, "If you're gonna take this job, you have to have a nose for news. Remember, always, always have a nose for news."

Thus, my days as a Personnel Specialist were truly "numbered" and I ended up spending less than a week in that position in Vietnam.

December 29, 1967

"Dearest Darling — I love you!"

"It's 9:20 pm"

"I doubt if you'd believe it, I might have an MOS (Military Occupational Specialty) change coming." ..... The reason for the change is simple - I'm no longer working in Personnel."

"This morning the Battalion Sergeant Major, the highest Enlisted Rank possible, called me into his office and told me he had an offer. I accepted - so I picked up my few possessions and moved into Battalion Headquarters. Of course, this is really no big change physically - Btn Hqts is only 50 yards (more or less) from Personnel. But - the position is somewhat more important."

"Beginning January 5th, I'll become the Public Information Specialist for the 43rd Sig Bn. I'll be in charge of all news releases (TV, radio, and newspapers), all correspondence with news media personnel, Sports Editor for the Brigade

paper, and Assoc. Editor for "The Unicorn," the Battalion newspaper. Needless to say, it's a big job — I'll also be doing all the photos and developing them in the MACV laboratory."

"I'll tell you more later on - in my next tape. I hope you've gotten the first two by now."

"Together we walk day by day. L D"

Once again, in the blink of an eye, Karma tapped me on the shoulder and my MOS changed from 19K10 -- Armor Crewman (at Fort Knox) to 71H20 -- Personnel Specialist (also at Fort Knox) to 71Q20 -- Reporter, Journalist, aka Information Specialist (in Pleiku).

At the outset, much of my time in this new position was spent "learning the ropes" while doing routine, mundane, humdrum office work, some of it not much different from what I would have been doing in the Personnel Office as a clerk. Eventually that would change to something more interesting and challenging, hard-core journalism and features writing. My days began with me typing out letters to wives, mothers, or other "specifically designated family member, next of kin." The letters, individually signed by the CO, informed them that their loved one "has arrived safely in Vietnam where they are serving an important role as a member of the 43rd Signal Battalion defending the freedom and liberty of the South Vietnamese in their struggle against Communist aggressors"… etc.

My office was located in "HQ," the Headquarters Building which housed our CO (Commanding Officer) Lieutenant Colonel Leo F. DuBeau, our XO (Executive Officer) Major Edward Raleigh, -- two really good men and great leaders in my opinion. My immediate supervisor, Captain Darrell Hott and Battalion Sergeant Major Golden (later SgtMaj Rogers) also had their offices in HQ. I eventually came to respect and admire all of these men who were very supportive of me in my new position.

S-1, Personnel: administrative head for assignments, processed awards, solved issues with pay, requested new troops as needed, and also addressed issues under UCMJ (Uniform Code of Military Justice). It was in a separate building near HQ.

S-2, Intelligence: in the opposite "wing" of our "C-shaped" building. S-2 kept data on enemy movement, strengths, and deployments and it also handled security clearances, maintained the battalion's Signal Operating Instructions and radio codes, and the battalion's map collection.

S-3, Training and Operations: S-3 scheduled and monitored training within all our units for our men who needed to update skills and knowledge about new communication equipment and systems. S-3 also was responsible for ammunition supply.

S-4, Supply: Supply was essentially in charge of all military materials. They handled inventory records, requests for new supplies and replacements for equipment damaged or destroyed in enemy attacks.

Along with clerical tasks, I monitored our HQ Radio which had the ability to link us to all our units. The radio equipment was mounted on a shelf just above and to the right of my desk. Answering radio calls was not a problem since I had received plenty of radio training in Armor School at Fort Knox. From time to time I would conduct radio checks with our outlying units and especially anyone traveling or working beyond our immediate perimeter to make sure communications with them remained "Five by Five," an expression meaning loud and clear. After all, we were a Communications Unit and communications by long line, radio and satellite were our first priority. Eventually, within a month or so, as fighting intensified around us and at our other more remote sites, when a unit came under attack, they would radio me and I would relay the messages to the appropriate section or officer. For security, no names were ever used, so the radio call sign for the Info Office was *Runner Prowler Six*. And just so the enemy couldn't identify him or know with whom we were communicating, the CO's call sign changed periodically. There was no Runner Prowler One. Another call sign used while I was stationed in Pleiku was "Saucy Ricketts." It was assigned to the 361st Signal at An Khe, while another call sign was "Blunt Spear." Many of these radio call signs were chosen in part because they likely would have been difficult for non-English-speaking Vietnamese to pronounce or to impersonate friendly forces' voices.

Chapter Seven

"The Times, They Are a-Changin"
Peter, Paul & Mary
(Written by Bob Dylan - 1964)

Mundane routines, observations, and excerpts from letters to Lynne.

None of the letters I wrote to Lynne revealed any information about what I was doing or what kinds of things were going on in my area of the Central Highlands. My communiques with her were love letters sent from a sad and lonely soldier -- a universal sentiment thousands of us were experiencing -- missing our dearest loved ones and families at home. Days and nights at the outset of my tour were filled with more routine tasks and many, many reports, while evenings at the NCO Club consisted of chatting, gossiping, listening to music, and drinking. A whole lot of drinking, sometimes described as excessive, went on in Vietnam and, sadly, eventually that turned into abuse of other substances for many troops. I'm happy to say, not for me.

I spent a few nights standing guard, usually inside a bunker on the north perimeter; we did not post foot sentries along this line. However, there were a handful of "foot sentries" along the wire paralleling the road that led to our entrance from MACV and the 71st Evacuation Hospital a short distance away. (My photo on the cover illustrates that.) But, along our most vulnerable perimeter, guards were posted in guard towers and bunkers. Guard duty was rotated among all members of the unit except for extremely vital duty communications operators and personnel whose daytime assignments were essential or strategic to unit operations. Those of us who worked in HQ often worked both days and nights, depending on what might be transpiring with our units spread across the Central Highlands. That duty automatically exempted us from any regularly scheduled guard duty. Therefore, other than when we were under attack, I was posted only three times for nighttime guard duty during my year in 'Nam.

On one of those nights, I was posted on Tropo Hill adjacent to our compound. My vantage point was a 20-foot-high tower that overlooked the corner of the 71st Evac and Pleiku Air Base in the distance. Shortly after midnight, a common time for attacks, the Viet Cong launched a mortar and rocket attack towards the airbase. As soon as that barrage started, I radioed in a report of what little I could see in the nearly-complete total darkness even though it was only about a mile and a half away (as the crow flies). The Tropo Hill Commander of the Relief (COR) was apparently flustered that I couldn't give them an accurate distance in the dark. In 1967-68 we did not have infrared or night vision equipment or "Starscopes." We had to rely solely on what we could see with our naked eyes. So the distance I gave them was just an "educated" guess.

I estimated the incoming rounds to be about 1500 to 2000 meters away and called that in. However, that seemed to confuse whoever was on duty. Since this was on Tropo Hill and not at the 43rd main compound, I wasn't familiar with individuals in their chain of command, so I had no idea with whom I was talking or who was manning the radio in the Command Bunker…other than perhaps some "nameless" COR.

The COR keyed the radio…and then there was a distinct pause. Finally, he asked, "Uh, what do you mean? How far is that**?**" I shook my head and thought to myself, "Don't they understand meters? Maybe I should tell them in yards." But I quickly changed my mind and decided to tell them the estimated distance was, "… about a mile or maybe a little more." Unfortunately, that didn't seem to help at all either. ("Who in the world was this dimwit manning the Command Post? I wondered.) I finally said, "They're dropping rounds East-Southeast of us about a mile away and marching them towards the airbase." This was intended to relay the message that the enemy was dropping mortar rounds in sequence along a particular path in the general direction of the airfield. Now, who wouldn't understand that?

Since the attack was directed away from us, and still a mile away, we were considered outside the action and the CP did not hit the "Chicken Switch" (siren) that would have put the entire area on alert. Instead, I got to stay in the tower and watch "the fireworks show" from my lofty vantage point.

The Viet Cong frequently conducted nighttime harassment shelling of all our bases, especially the airbase. They hoped to cause some disruption by damaging buildings, perhaps even hitting one of the aircraft which were sheltered in revetments. If they were lucky, they might inflict a few casualties, hit an ammo bunker (aka dump) or at least, punch holes in the runways.

"B Flight," 4th Air Commando Squadron had four AC-47 "Spooky" gunships stationed at the airstrip. One of these took off, circled not too far from my vantage point, then opened up on the suspected mortar positions. It was a sight and sound to behold with multiple streams of fire and a harsh brrrrrrrrrrrrruuuuuuuuttt (a fairly high-pitched buzz or whirring sound) from its triple mini-guns. Flares were also dropped to light up the area and suspected enemy position; they drifted down slowly under their swaying parachutes.

The darkness of the night while on guard duty, especially on a moonless or cloudy night really bothered me. I know that kind of tension pushed virtually everyone to the brink. In the incredible blackness you squinted into the darkness looking for any hint of movement. You listened, trying to determine if "that" noise was a normal rustle of the grass or someone crawling towards you a few inches at a time? Was "that" the sound of wind shaking the metal and stone-filled beer and soda cans we hung along portions of our barbed wire perimeter? Or, did someone bump against the wire or catch their clothing on it trying to penetrate the perimeter fencing? The latter was a bit unlikely since Sappers (bomb and satchel charge carrying commandos) often wore little other than a loin cloth to avoid just that type of thing. Or, did "Charlie" somehow crawl through one of the numerous tunnels dug near our perimeter, pop up and turn one of our Claymore mines toward us, so if they were tripped, they'd send 700 deadly 1/8th inch steel balls ripping through the area?

Compounding this foreboding suspense were the seasonal spells of fog or rain or both. Hunkered under a poncho, your tense and weary body shivering, trying to keep your weapon protected from the elements -- but always at the ready – emphatically compounded the strain.

Unknowing, eerie, frightening, night guard held the suspense of a horror movie — but worse, it was real life.

Later in the year, standing guard duty on the perimeter of the compound ended for me. Instead, I was called upon to be "Commander of the Relief," the NCO in charge of all the nighttime sentries on duty. That duty was carried out in the Command Post and I found it was much easier and certainly less stressful for my by-now-frazzled nerves.

---0---

January 1st, 1968

> *"I believe that this is, perhaps, the best way to begin a New Year.*
>   *I love, love, love thee*
>   *and to thee pledge my life*
>   *forever."*

"As per usual, there's nothing going on here. For the last week I've had nary a drop of alcohol (including last night). So, you can see that I really didn't usher in the New Year as we did a year ago—Remember? I doubt if you'd forget New Year's Eve in the living room. Hope you all had an enjoyable holiday."

"Christmas was spent doing nothing, save for the tape I sent thee. New Year's Eve was spent in the office and today I got off 2 hours early, came back to the barracks, laid down a while. Now — here we are."

"Graffiti from a latrine here:
'Ko Texas is where the action is.' (the "as" letters in Texas were crossed off) *(and below it) 'Kotex is out. Tampax is in.'"*

The walls of latrines were the proverbial, unofficial, community bulletin board for sophomoric jokes and graffiti. While latrines were nothing new to me since I frequently had used outhouses in the campo in South America, they were somewhat different in Vietnam. In South America we had "single holers" where you would simply sit to do your business but put the soiled toilet paper (or whatever you had available) in a bin next to the latrine or outhouse. Then that paper would be destroyed by burning. In Vietnam, latrines were built in the traditional style – plain wood frame -- but here they were a "multi-hole" affair, affording absolutely no privacy whatsoever. The prevailing attitude was, "GI-GO-GO" (a play-on-words poking fun at "Go-Go Dancers" of the time.) And, sometimes our diets and other circumstances forced us to really go-go-go.

A more significant difference was that in Vietnam there was no "pit" underneath the latrines. Instead, a series of 50-gallon drums were cut in half and placed on the ground underneath each hole. Daily, these would be pulled outside, doused with a combination of gasoline and kerosene or diesel fuel, then set ablaze. This conflagration sent noxious black smoke billowing into the air. The Vietnamese thought this was an awful waste of valuable fertilizer since they spread this kind of stuff as nutrients for their crops. Additionally, burning latrine crap used up a large amount of diesel fuel and gasoline, another "waste" of resources.

The job of "Shit Burning Detail" was generally assigned to a lower-rank enlisted man, sometimes as punishment. Other times it was contracted to Vietnamese civilians. Vietnamese civilians were desperate to get clearance to work on base. And for this particular job it was steady work - steady pay – every day. Also, contrasted to local work, which likely was nonexistent in the first place, these jobs paid fairly well.

GI's were discouraged from urinating "while seated" in the latrines since that made the offensive, wet mess harder to burn. Instead, some other options were possible: outdoor "piss tubes" (simply emptying into the ground, or depending on how hurriedly they had been constructed, emptying into something akin to a stone-filled dry well). These were set up behind a short wall near the latrine. Sometimes they were installed closer to important work areas such as Comm Center or Operations. Of course, very large bases had modern toilets and sophisticated waste management systems. But there was no such thing as a septic or sewer system in these early, hastily established base compounds or at any of our remote outlying sites.

January 3rd, 1968

"Sorry I didn't write last nite but, once again we worked late, finishing up the R & A for this quarter. R & A stands for Review and Analysis - a report published quarterly & composed of 75-120 pages. It's really nasty cutting the stencils for each page but, it goes to press (mimeo) tomorrow - hopefully."

"So now I've tackled another project. One of our buildings here in the compound is used for meetings, Chapel, & movies (almost every night). Beginning tonite I became one of the projectionists, working every other evening. The projector (singular) is a small 16mm. We did have two, but one was returned to the states for repairs. The job doesn't pay anything so I'm doing it as a favor."

---0---

A little Fort Knox backstory ... Before leaving for Vietnam, I had worked part time on weekends as a projectionist at the Waybur Theatre at Fort Knox. The major difference between being a projectionist at the Waybur versus the Chapel was that at the Waybur we had a pair of very large, commercial Carbon Arc Projectors. In contrast, the 16mm projector in Vietnam was much smaller and easier to operate. Additionally, those large Carbon Arc projectors at Fort Knox were a bit tricky to synchronize.

Standard Hollywood films were much too long to store or to ship on a single reel so they were shipped in multiple 24-inch reels (usually 4 or 5), approximately 1000 feet of film on each. In order to switch from one reel to another, you had to watch the screen carefully for the first cue, normally a dot or series of oval shapes — about 17-24 minutes in, then light and adjust the arc on the second projector and prepare for the final cue to make the changeover. The arc-rod was simply a special welding rod inside the projector housing. Even though it was on "auto-advance," it needed near-constant attention and adjusting so the film didn't appear to flicker. Next, you had to watch the screen for a second series of black or white dots in the upper right corner of the frame. When they appeared, you switched the "changeover douser" on the first projector with one hand and opened the same mechanism on the second projector with your other hand. If you missed the dots you were likely to get the timing wrong and the GIs in the theater gave you the "business" with yells, whistles, a few obscenities, and cat calls.

I remember that happening only one time as a projectionist at the Waybur. We were showing a double feature: *The Fortune Cookie* starring Jack Lemmon and Walter Matthau plus *It's a Bikini World* starring former "Mouseketeer" Tommy Kirk. During a reel change in *It's a Bikini World*, I saw the first cue but forgot to switch the "changeover douser," at the right time. The sound continued playing but the screen was totally black, leading the GIs in the audience to think I was censoring the skimpy bikini parts. My supervisor, Staff Sergeant John Knox (yes, that was his name…funny coincidence) quickly reminded me to flip the douser and all was well, save for a handful of catcalls and whistles and my embarrassment…well hidden from view in the projection booth high above the audience.

One other note, in addition to watching the movie for free as a projectionist at the Waybur, I was paid $4.80 for a single feature and $3.90 more if it was a double feature. No extra for cartoons or trailers.

January 6, 1968

"I got 11 of the first 17 letters (you wrote) yesterday. It was absolutely fabulous hearing from you. Also got a note from Mom & Dad K and the Ws. Thank them for me please. OK?"

"There are a thousand things I want to say, but it's 7:30 am and I must go to work. So, I'll write a big long letter (if I can) tonight. We'll see."

"I wept a bit last night - a candle's glow can shine for thousands and thousands of miles when fanned by the breezes of love. It's warm and comforting and when combined with desire - to love, cherish, honor, and obey & remain faithful, - it's the brightest light 'neath the stars above.' "Indeed, it is brighter than the brightest star itself. Yes, I wept a bit last night - because I know that with the patience and love we share, someday soon, together we shall sit beside that candle & love & feel the warmth of love in us."

Weeping? Poetic license or real tears? Likely some of both. I know I had wept a few times during my first days in South America. After all, I was away from home for the first time in my life, alone in a jungle where no one spoke English. But this was entirely different. Here raw feelings could be exposed in the blink of an eye. And once again, I found myself on new, uncharted, and precarious ground -- thrust physically, mentally, and emotionally into an unfamiliar, threatening and potentially deadly environment.

At the outset of my tour there actually were very few signs of fighting around us -- save for periodic booming salvos from the 52nd Artillery Group's 8-inch howitzers on "Artillery Hill" about a mile or so to our North-Northwest. We could hear the reverberating sounds of the blasts from the muzzles and sometimes the whoosh of shells overhead, but we rarely heard the explosions when the ordinance impacted -- as far as 18 miles away. So, in many respects, the war itself didn't seem to be a real issue, at least not for us in Pleiku. Plus, I was traveling more than I ever realized I would be, and though my home base was at the 43rd HHD in Pleiku, my work locations seemed to change a day or two at a time, even after arriving at my "permanent assignment" at the 43rd . It would be about three weeks before the unmistakable bitter reality of this place would set in.

Tuesday, January 10, 2:45 pm

This day I found myself writing to Lynne from Nha Trang at 21st Signal Group Headquarters. I was there likely delivering the R & A Report I had mentioned in a letter to Lynne a week earlier. With my new MOS, my Security Clearance moved from Secret to Top Secret almost immediately. With that high-level clearance, I began to travel as a Courier between our unit and 21st Signal Group on the coast in Nha Trang, and 1st Signal Brigade in Long Binh about an hour Northeast of Saigon.

This day I also wrote about sending money home to Lynne but… *"I still haven't been able to get any Money Orders. They seem to be in short supply. So, I'm going over to finance to have another allotment made out to you for $150 per month."*

"Today I decided to buy a camera. It's a Topcon RE Super - the best they make. It cost $150 (at the PX)."

The Topcon eventually became the camera I used throughout my tour for both personal and Army assignments. It was a great bargain since it retailed for nearly $400 in civilian stores at home.

I wrote dozens of poems in the love letters I sent to Lynne during my time in Vietnam. I handwrote these on any scrap of paper I could find, from lined legal yellow pad, to tissue-thin, plain airmail sheets, and even on the back of 43rd Signal worship service bulletins. I composed the first of these on the second Sunday in January. On that same day I also wrote the following on a separate, small plain sheet from a notepad:

January 14, 1968

"Dearest Love, My eyes are tiring, my body almost weak, my hand unsteady. But I must not rest until I have told thee, in part, of a story - glorious as the first hue of rose-dawn."

"How does one begin such an enormous task; that of telling thee of all my love for thee - alone? Aye, indeed, it is all but impossible, for, who could scan the heavens and count every star or drink of a wine skin and taste <u>every</u> drop? Who could even read one word and be sure of its entire meaning, its complete text? Nary a soul living - save God. And is it not of Him we speak?"

"Perhaps if a word were able - God - Love - the word written or spoken, sung, heard, known. Perhaps if I lived a hundred years and few fold. Nay, even then it could never be complete."

"Thus, must I solely, inadequately tell thee of a part …. Not enough I'm afraid - but truly honest and from my yearning heart —

>   *I love thee —*
>   *and love thee —*
>   *and love thee. Forever, D"*

Then just eight days later…

January 22, 1968
"I've been sitting in Cam Ranh Bay for the past 6 1/2 hours and before that, 4 1/2 hours at Pleiku Air Base. It's 1:05 am."

Trips like this became a surprisingly common occurrence in my job, but I simply cannot recall, nor did I mention the purpose of my assignment in the note hastily scribbled in the wee hours of the morning. The trips were too frequent to remember and, as mentioned before, I wrote absolutely nothing at all to explain or describe the assignments I was on. I'm certain that was due to their confidential nature and I took my Top-Secret clearance in absolute earnest. Instead, I wrote page after page of my desperate longing and intense love for my wife.

"Devotion is a strange creature. I guess there's a tiny bit in everyone - be it just an inclination to breathe or, at some time inhale while thinking about it. Some even have a deeper emotion; something makes them twinge at a thought - and a word like "crackling" when describing the brisk air of a chilly morning, or the sun's rays across the frosted and glazed snow of early winter. That happened. Not too terribly long ago I met someone devoted to life."

"Because of a breath, a hastily written note, I now love … or perhaps it's that I understand it more."

"Twas' far away - can't recall exactly when but was a couple a' years in an office when I read the mail - little there was and someone offered the phrase, "this tired bit of humanity" and I returned the gesture by denying their desire to that note denying existence."

"Denying, denied. Perhaps too few sacrifices are made these days - 'cept by a couple 'a folk. So few, so very few."

"So, I packed my bags and returned to the world - eager while hesitant and wondering, tired yet fresh and a bit more full of some vitality I lacked before the original journey."

"Somehow it never occurred to me that there was life on this Earth. I just naturally (or perhaps unnaturally) assumed every color was graying. How many temples attest to that?"

"How fresher the smells of auburn autumn now! How colored the spring - vibrant! How cozy the leeward side of a summer cliff and warm the winter fire!"

"To thee - my entire life and the love I possess - all - to eternity, I pledge thee alone."

January 28, 1968

"This time it's Pleiku where I sit, waiting, the sun's overpowering heat burning the stones around the bench where I sit - wilting. It's sort of strange; at nite one needs extra blankets or a jacket if going outside, and at times, that isn't enough; and the light hours are filled with heat and dust and the smell of scorched roadway."

"The bugs and flying insects are outrageous - flies, gnats, and mosquitoes are constantly harassing you - they even go as far as invading the privacy of one's own locker or bunk or ear."

"The dust leaves not one item untouched, uncovered, unscarred. It is so finely ground that one has trouble sweeping with a straw broom so you use a Vietnamese-made reed broom with "bristles" as thin as the silk on an ear of corn. Everything, at times, will not brush away this curse of erosion."

"Come March or April I'll complain again. The monsoons will trickle one day for an hour, then for two hours, and then for months without a let-up. I'll probably then wish for dust. A vicious circle of sorts, non?"

"And all this time - I have and shall think of green and leaves, snow and cool summer breezes; that quiet nite on the patio - the smell of mock-orange on the wind or the smoke from a charcoal stove whispering by."

"I'm looking out past the gate - towards "Tropo Hill" and the compound. There's a spiraling column of reddish-brown swirling upward from the ground to place it somewhere else for a moment. Then to snatch it away once more."

"I stop to wipe the sweat from my brow and glance towards some children sitting nearby. Their clothes are ragged and dirty - I guess you'd call them clothes. And they've collected some empty soda cans and are building a "castle." Too bad, they'll never live in anything as good as a "pop can castle." Too bad, they'll probably sleep right there tonight, on that piece of cardboard under that dying young palm. It never had a chance."

The next few days would prove to be unequivocally significant for me and indeed, for everyone involved in the war. And it wouldn't only be reddish dust devils swirling into the Vietnam skies.

Chapter Eight

"We Gotta Get Outta This Place"
The Animals
(Written by Mann and Weil - 1965)
[Undoubtedly the most requested song in my repertoirè]

1968 - Year of the Monkey and the Tet Offensive
Năm Con Khỉ và Sự kiện Tết Mậu Thân 1968

The Vietnamese Lunar New Year or "Tet" is the biggest and most important holiday in Vietnamese culture. It's a time for pilgrimages to the graves of ancestors, and visits to homes for large family gatherings with special meals. It has been likened to having Thanksgiving, Christmas, and New Year's all rolled into one extended holiday event. Thus, we, like everyone else in country, were lulled into a state of inattentiveness in anticipation of a ceasefire during this special time. U.S. Ambassdor Ellsworth Bunker and President of the Republic of Vietnam Nguyen Van Thieu met to discuss what to do. They, along with General William Westmoreland, issued a joint 36-hour cease-fire. The NVA and Viet Cong announced their own 7-day cease-fire. So, US Forces tacitly accepted that premise since the enemy had used the Tet ceasefire to redeploy and resupply their troops in previous years. They had not used this holy time for widespread attacks.

That is, until now.

It soon became all too obvious and all too late that the North Vietnamese Army (NVA, aka PAVN – People's Army of Vietnam) along with the Viet Cong (VC) had an altogether different plan this year. Their highly complex and multi-phase plan was code-named *Ngày lễ* or "N-Day," a name mimicking the massive Allied "D-Day" invasion of France during WWII. The NVA and VC would essentially violate their own announced ceasefire in an extensive country-wide series of surprise, destructive, and deadly attacks.

I had been in country now just about a month and a half when at 2:00 am on January 30, 1968, our compound was attacked by elements of the North Vietnamese 95 B Regiment and the Viet Cong 200th Artillery. The war, unquestionably, had arrived "up close and personal," landing in our figurative laps!

The shelling with mortars and Soviet-made 122 mm rockets caught us completely off guard -- even though US SIGINT (signal intelligence intercepted January 13, 15, 16, and 17) had indicated there might be an attack in our area of the Central Highlands around this time. Unfortunately, those reports and others commenting on a build-up of NVA 1st Division and 24th Regiment enemy troops in the Tri-Border (Vietnam, Cambodia, and Laos), an area roughly 80 miles to our northwest, were doubted or simply ignored. And so, the US and ARVN forces planned on a holiday, where in fact, many ARVN soldiers had actually returned to their homes for the celebrations.

I was sound asleep when an earth-shaking, booming, and startling "karummp" shook our barracks, raining dust and debris down from walls and ceilings. It was the first impact and explosion of a series of enemy rockets and mortars aimed at our compound. That first rocket hit and exploded about halfway between our barracks and the north perimeter a hundred-plus yards away. Fortunately, it missed our ammo bunker which was hit in a much-later attack, but nevertheless it left a hole six feet deep and nearly eight feet across. The blast sent small pieces of shrapnel and chunks of red clay whistling across the area. The explosion and more that followed were deafening, stunning me and literally rattling me out of my bunk. Sirens began to wail, their piercing screech accompanied by more explosions from mortars landing in and around the compound as well as around Tropo Hill.

It took me a few seconds to realize this was not the usual booming noise from Artillery Hill that I had grown accustomed to hearing. This was something quite different and unmistakably much closer. I grabbed my flak jacket, helmet, and rifle hanging on the wall by the door and bolted out of the room. I scrambled in a semi-crouch, ducking below the window line. My untied boot laces slapped the floor with a random, mocking sound as I darted down the short hall and outside to the nearest bunker at the end of our *hooch*. The air was filled with smoke and the acrid smell of exploded ordinance. As we knelt low, we pressed our bodies against the sandbagged walls, and we heard pieces of shrapnel hitting the sides of the building. We could feel the reverberations of repeated explosions -- some falling short of our perimeter defenses, others pummeling the Pleiku Airbase to our southeast. Small arms and machine gun fire rattled off buildings and hills in the distance, seemingly coming from nearly every direction and even from Pleiku City where elements of the North Vietnamese 95 B Regiment and VC 407 and 408 Sapper Battalions were penetrating the city limits. The attacks on us and on Pleiku were the initial attacks of the extensive, country-wide Tet Offensive. The second NVA and VC "main thrust" would come a day later when almost 100 more provincial and district towns plus Saigon and Hue would be attacked simultaneously.

A pause in the shelling afforded us an opportunity to sprint from the safety of the bunker to our assigned defensive positions on the perimeter. Normal nighttime guards were already posted along the perimeter in machine gun bunkers and on several watchtowers. Flares lit up the area, slowly swinging down under their parachutes, or arching across the open fields to our north, above the Montagnard village west of us, and around the Pleiku Airfield to our southeast. Some of these were ground-launched while others were dropped by aircraft circling the area. Their pseudo-festive display lent a bizarre aura to this ominous and abrupt start of the holiday.

From our position on the line we could hear the reverberating booms and see flashes of "outgoing" rounds from the 52nd Artillery Group on Artillery Hill. They were raining fire on the enemy positions that spotters had now identified.

The shelling eventually subsided as we anxiously waited, nerves on edge. A few tense hours later, a siren sounded the all clear.

That siren turned out to be a rather clumsy mistake. While it appeared the return artillery and gunship fire had silenced the enemy for the time being, they were simply waiting patiently. The NVA and VC knew our troops would be walking back to our hootches when that loud "all clear" siren was sounded. Thus, almost as soon as the siren went off, mortars began dropping around our compound again. We ran back to our defensive positions where, this time, we stayed until daylight. Sometime after sunrise, Command sent down a directive to pass along the all-clear via word of mouth. And, while we should have had phone communications between bunkers and our battle Command Bunker - located behind the S1 building – the wires had been strung between poles and were knocked out sometime during the initial barrage. Those communication lines would eventually be buried safely underground.

There were times when we were in the perimeter bunkers during or shortly after attacks when we got to watch "Spooky" circling the area near Lake Bien Hoa north of us. Biên Hô means "Sea Lake" but it's also known by its Vietnamese name *T'Nung* and *Ea Nueng*, "Sea on the Mountain." *Chi Ho Me* is the first and closest short peak east of the northern edge of the lake and only a few miles from our vantage point. Beyond it, the *Không Grang* Mountains provided an incalculable number of hiding places for the enemy, so it was a favorable, albeit difficult target for our gunships which included a number of different fighter-bombers aircraft based with the 6th Air Commando Squadron at Pleiku Air Base. One of them, the Douglas A-1E "Skyraider" was a memorable prop-driven attack aircraft that honestly sounded to me like a giant version of one of my dad's old farm tractors…except that when it taxied by or flew low overhead the "puttering" sound of their engine was deafening!

Spooky was the nickname for a specially outfitted AC-47 gunship. It was the military version of the DC-3, the extremely reliable cargo plane similar to the ones I had been on as a passenger numerous times in South America. The big difference between the two versions was that

Spooky, aka *Puff the Magic Dragon*, was outfitted like no other plane. It literally lit up the area with streams of fire from its three 7.62 mm General Electric miniguns. The guns were mounted through two rear window openings and the side cargo door on the pilot's side, the port or left side of the airplane. Each gun was actually a six-barrel rotary machine gun capable of firing 2,000 to 6,000 rounds per minute. They were absolutely devastating and utterly fascinating to watch. The tracers in the belts of ammunition were armor-piercing incendiary rounds. They were spaced every 5th shell and looked like ragged red lines of liquid fire reaching from the sky to the ground. Periodically we also could see a few scraggly lines of ineffective green enemy tracers being fired in the opposite direction. Green tracers were the color of VC and NVA small arms ammunition while red tracers were universally used by US and Australian Forces.

Following an attack one night, the all-clear was passed along and we began making our way back to our barracks. Suddenly, and without any warning, a series of tremendously loud explosions occurred. Oddly, they seemed to come from almost directly overhead and we dove for cover in the nearest ditch. Yet, no debris fell on or around us. The warning sirens blared immediately because guards on watch thought the attack had been renewed and we had additional incoming rockets or mortars.

A lull occurred and we ran back to our defensive positions on the north perimeter. Then, when no additional impacts occurred in or anywhere near the compound, word was passed along that the sounds likely came from a specially outfitted gunship, in this case a C130 rather than the older AC-47. The booming noise was made by one of the large cannons carried onboard, possibly the L60 Bofors 40mm cannon or the 105 mm M102 Howitzer. Both of these weapons were designed as artillery for ground use but were creatively adapted to the now-specially outfitted C130. When we realized there actually was no incoming, the all clear was passed along one more time.

Running to the perimeter and fighting bunkers could be in and of itself, a bit hazardous. The ground was bare and uneven in places. Twisting an ankle or knee was commonplace. Falling into a deep fighting trench along the line occurred to a handful of careless or luckless friends. Additionally, the entire area was littered with debris from the exploded shells or clods of dirt from the explosions during an attack.

Some drainage ditches lined one side of the rutted dirt road that led to my assigned position near the center of the north perimeter. So, between shell bursts during one of the attacks, Frank Swegheimer -- a great friend and barracks-roommate who worked just down the hall for our CO -- and I began to run towards our bunker positions near the wire. As we ran, we heard the telltale whistling-whooshing sound of an incoming rocket, and we immediately dove in unison for the nearest ditch. Aiming for the same spot, Frank landed just a second before me and, unfortunately, his rifle hit me in the mouth as I landed hard in the narrow depression. The resultant whack in the mouth gave me a fat lip and knocked out a piece of one of my teeth.

Dreams, Visions, and Nightmares --
A Never-Ending Skirmish in My Mind.

Our compound generally was harassed at night with rocket and mortar rounds, and we never experienced a ground assault while I was there. So, most of us were back in our offices during daylight hours albeit on modified alert. That meant extra guards and lookouts along the perimeter and manning the towers during Tet. Meanwhile, everyone else on duty at the motor pool, comm centers, mess hall, etc. were ready to move to the perimeter at a moment's notice.

Daytime operations at HHD during this period appeared to be moving along normally, yet there remained an underlying sense of uneasiness that everyone felt.

February 2, 1968

I was sitting at my desk in the HHD Information Office and beginning to compile information about our units' involvements across the highlands. Suddenly the radio on the wall next to me crackled and I heard, *"Runner Prowler, Runner Prowler,* this is_____; we are under attack." I responded with their call sign and, "This is Runner *Prowler Six.* Will relay. Wait one." I quickly ran down the hall toward the Commander's office to alert him and S2 (Intelligence) to tune to C Company's frequency and take over.

A short while later, I heard the sad and upsetting details about the Kontum attacks and the KIAs and WIAs from our unit.

The two men who lost their lives in these initial attacks were Sp4 Rich Gideon, a Personnel Specialist from Valley Stream, New York, and Sp4 Joe Rodrigues, a cook from Santa Rosa, California. Here is a brief excerpt from a note written to me by James (Monterey Jack) Mahan, a friend in C Company who, although wounded multiple times, repeatedly risked his own life to help his buddies and defend the compound. (Jack eventually was medivac-ed.)

> Jack: *"Tower Four was a mess, a sniper shot Rich in the back of the head and it took several of us to man-handle him down to the ground by human chain. There was blood all over the place and it stayed there for months."*

For four days NVA and Viet Cong threw absolutely everything they could at our men in Kontum including rockets, mortars, small arms, sappers carrying satchel charges, and even mortar rounds of tear gas. They eventually breached the wire of our compound in two places but were repelled repeatedly.

Jack recounted that one of the shells, *"either an RPG* (Rocket-Propelled Grenade) *or a shell from a recoilless rifle went through one of the support legs of the tower plus two feet of sandbags and exploded inside the bunker killing Joe."*

I visited C Company compound in Kontum along with our CO and Frank Swegheimer about two weeks after the initial attacks. Even at that time the tower remained a horrible sight with blood-stained ladder rungs and walls spattered with dried but unmistakable dark stains. Today, more than 50 years later, Frank tells me he still has vivid memories of this gruesome scene while I have totally blacked those images out of my mind and only recall the scene with PTSD-numbness when looking at the photos I took. The view through the guard tower gun ports, the completely devastated, shot-up buildings, trees with their branches shattered, the entirely flattened Prisoner Interrogation Center across the road where the enemy repeatedly attacked our men evoke a horrible blackness I refuse to revisit.

Eventually wooden walls were installed around the ladders to block the enemy's view. But I continue to have disturbing visions of Rich and Joe both getting hit. And the details of that firefight, recounted to me by close friends, is a recurring revenant that simply cannot be erased from my subconscious.

Rich was the very first KIA whose name I recognized. His death has flashed repeatedly in and out of my memory in gruesome detail. Sadly, his and Joe's deaths are indelibly linked to that first enemy attack radio call I answered. And I cannot begin to tell you how many times I've mentally climbed up and down that ladder …. and realize I am completely powerless to do anything at all.

Chapter Nine

"Twist & Shout"
The Isley Brothers
(Written by Phil Medley and Bert Berns - 1962)

The attacks during Tet were the bona fide genesis of my work as a journalist for the US Army. During the days, weeks, and for several months thereafter, my desk duties remained unchanged. However, my travel to our signal sites in other parts of the Central Highlands increased significantly thereby delaying those normal office duties for short periods of time.

February 15, 1968

A totally unexpected surprise came my way on Thursday, February 15 when the men of HHD and Company A were ordered to fall into formation. As soon as they were assembled, Captain Darrell Hott, Battalion Adjutant, called me forward. There, LTC DuBeau presented me with the Army Commendation Medal for my work at Fort Knox. The award was the first of three ACMs I would eventually receive during my time in the Army. (The second two, Bronze Oak Leaf Clusters for exceptional meritorious service, were awarded for my work in Vietnam and at Fort Ord.) This first award was recommended and forwarded to the Department of the Army by the Office of the Adjutant General, US Army Armor Center, Fort Knox. In part it read, *"Specialist Four Kaltreider demonstrated exceptional ability and untiring efforts..." ... (his) ..."ability to grasp situations and take immediate, decisive action with a minimum amount of guidance was a key factor in his efficiently coordinating and effecting the administrative functions of his branch."*

Two other men, Staff Sergeant Levi Sanders and my friend, SP5 Frank Swegheimer each received awards at this ceremony for their previous service; Sanders from the 5th Infantry Division and Swegheimer from XVIII Airborne Corps.

A month later I would be covering ceremonies at other sites like Kontum and An Khe where our men would be receiving much more significant awards for service under quite different circumstances -- action and valor under fire and some for wounds received in those engagements.

February 19, 1968

Another brief note to Lynne contained only one simple line: *"I'm driving to Kontum to cover the fighting."*

By now the heaviest fighting of the Tet Offensive had decreased significantly. Nevertheless, we went to visit several of our more remote sites so our CO personally could assess firsthand what was going on. He also used these visits to present the first of many awards to men of the 43rd Signal Battalion for their service and gallantry under fire. These visits allowed him to meet face-to-face with our guys who had been through so much across the Central Highlands. And while all of our units were subjected to vicious enemy attacks, one unit in particular defended their compound against repeated vicious and deadly attacks. Our men were communications experts, called upon to maintain viable, effective and clear communications for all allied forces regardless of the fierce fighting, yet they also were compelled to defend their compound from repeated enemy assaults. They did both with determination, courage, and honor.

---0---

A verbatim transcription of one of the articles published in our unit newspaper (as well as sent "up the chain" to 1st Signal Brigade and Army IO) begins on the next page. This news account is fairly descriptive of the assault and firefight on our Company C compound during the Tet Offensive. In reality, the details of the fight were much more gruesome, but we did not publish anything like that or in the style of "tabloid" journalism.

The following article became the lead headline for the March 1968 edition of *The Unicorn*, published about a month after the fact. Many more articles would follow that included highlights about the incredibly brave men of C Company as well as other units and individuals with whom I had the honor of serving. Those kinds of stories were the essence of my job: human interest, morale building, and stories filled with words of encouragement.

You may notice that the following article carefully avoids mention of casualties, save for briefly mentioning Jack Mahan's wounds. For the record, the official casualty count in our unit from these fierce attacks was 2 KIA and 26 WIA.

---0---

"43rd Under Fire"
"Company C Repels Vicious Drive"

Editor's Note: The following account of the Tet Offensive Activities in and around the Kontum area of the Central Highlands is taken from an interview with Captain James Paisley, Commanding Officer, Company C, 43rd Signal Battalion (SPT), Kontum.

On the evening of January 29, 1968, the sounds of firecrackers, the smell of burning incense and the voices of joyful people filled the air around the Central Highland city of Kontum, Vietnam. What was supposed to be a period of contemplation, resolution-making, partying and celebration was about to become a bloodied page of history filled with some of the most awesome acts of terrorism the world has ever seen. And what was supposed to commemorate the arrival of the Lunar New Year, "The Year of the Monkey", was about to become the "Day of Defeat" for the forces of NVA and Viet Cong that had earlier infiltrated the mountains and jungles surrounding Kontum.

The celebrations had begun the afternoon of the 29th as a brilliant sun greeted the sound and laughter of children playing in the dusty and unpaved streets of the city, but before sunset the same day, the sky over this town had tuned pink with the color of tracers that ominously foretold of what was about to turn into the "Tet Offensive."

At midnight a stillness and quiet crept over Kontum. No voices were heard and no more firecrackers exploded. Guards on their posts squinted into the darkness of the moonless, starless night. A few men, clad only in their underwear, sensed that something was "in the air" and began to move equipment to the bunkers.

At two o'clock on the morning of the 30th, mortar rounds began to zero in on the town. The "thump and crunch" of the "incoming" came closer and closer to Charlie Company, 43rd Signal Battalion, the Northern-most American installation in Kontum. By four am the mortar rounds had "walked" their way down the road from the city and were heavily bombarding the "C" Company compound. Sniper fire from outside the perimeter smashed into the buildings and bunkers and ricocheted off of the metal supports of the radio towers. Flares lit the surrounding area while dragon ships and the constant fire from "Puff" riddled the enemy who had crept within fifty meters of the obstacles around the compound. The siege lasted throughout the seemingly endless night and throughout the following day. This harassing rain of fire from snipers, mortars, and artillery was almost perpetual.

Two tanks were moved inside the perimeter on the evening of February 2, the day of the heaviest fighting. Earlier that day the "PIC", Prisoner Interrogation Center, was taken over by the enemy and provided them with a concealed sniper position. The Tea Plantation on the South-West side and ARVN VIP quarters also provided positions for snipers and mortar teams. Small arms fire from Communist - made automatic weapons pinned C Company down with murderous crossfire while mortars peppered the area with a thundering barrage. Two towers were hit and the perimeter was breached. PFC James Mahan volunteered to go from the CP bunker to help reinforce the Eastern perimeter. While the enemy repeatedly raked the area with a wall of fire, he and two unidentified members of the 578th Signal Company quickly moved to a cinderblock bunker near the sector of the perimeter that had been breached. Showing little concern for his own safety yet realizing the necessity of holding the ground PFC Mahan cleared up the area with accurate and sustained fire. Although wounded in the leg and chest, he continued to maintain his position until the area was secure.

At almost the same time, SSG Raymond Ross saw that tower four was coming under heavy attack. SSG Ross volunteered to go to the aid of the men in the tower and stayed all day and night. He was knocked out of the tower several times but refused to quit his position. His accurate, intense fire aided immeasurably in holding the area.

On the third day of the fighting Charlie Company was hit with a different type of harassment. The VC/NVA began to pour mortar rounds into the area as they had done previously. But suddenly the cry, "Gas! Tear gas attack!," went up. Quickly donning their masks, the men of C Company foiled the attempt of the enemy to demoralize and debilitate temporarily those defending the compound.

The enemy wasn't the only one to "get in some licks." ARVN artillery was right on the spot with VT, a high-explosive round that explodes about 40 feet in the air and spreads its death-dealing shrapnel in a wide circle. Air support, as described by Captain Paisley, was, "Fabulous. There were strikes by F4 Phantoms, Skyraiders, and helicopter gunships."

"The VC/NVA objective was to move through the C Company area, through the MACV compound, and onto Corps Headquarters. However, Charlie Company, assuming the role of Infantry as well as Signal Men, blunted the attack and stopped the drive." The estimated body count outside the perimeter totaled over 250 enemy dead.

"There was so much to do and so much happening that you had no time to be worried or scared. You just had to be busy," continued Captain Paisley. Specialist Four Charles Riley was one of the busiest. After noting that some of the commo gear had been knocked out, SP Riley rerouted circuits and pieced together equipment from different sets, keeping Company C "on the air" throughout the attack.

Another member who was kept extremely busy was mess steward SSG St Julian who saw that there was at least one hot meal per day for the men. Both SSG St Julian and the cooks did an outstanding job. But, of course, this is true of all the men. "C Company came through."

The largest part of the offensive lasted for seven days. Only occasional sniper fire broke the stillness after that.

By the 10th of February, the rebuilding was done and almost everything was back to normal. Communication lines that had been snipped by the VC were now buried, a new tower built, foxholes placed around the compound and full communications restored. The Tet Offensive was over, the VC/NVA drive halted. The quiet that was once commonplace in Kontum had returned to the dusty and pock-marked street of the Highland city defended in the highest tradition of the United States Army by the officers and men of Charlie Company, 43rd Signal Battalion.

---0---

Immediately following the attacks, I did not get to interview PFC Mahan in person since he had been airlifted by Medivac helicopter due to his injuries. However, I have had frequent, almost weekly contact with "Monterey Jack" Mahan since beginning to write this book. Over the course of the past year, he has shared many more personal and painful details about these attacks and, in fact, other incidents where we both lost mutual friends. I am extremely grateful to him for his help in dealing with the mental struggles I (indeed, we both) have endured. I wish him a safe and secure future and complete, lasting healing. Below is an excerpt from some of the communications we've shared. It is indicative of the "raw material" I gathered as an Information Specialist then used to write stories and news releases similar to the one you just read.

DK: *"Jack, how in the hell did you do it? What was it like being under such intense pressure and nearly constant enemy fire?"*

JM: *"Denny, I always felt like I was just there and had very little control over things. In the end I just tried to be ready for the unexpected. Numb was what I felt most of the time from September '67 till August '68. I can't recall how I felt the first half dozen contacts. I just didn't know what to do, part panic and curiosity."*

"I was sent to Dak To in late October to supply our team up there just as the hill battles started. Came back a week later in shock from the power of the NVA battering the base. We were sniped at a few times on the road but got back OK. A week later they sent me back up with another transmitter and ammo. We lost three engineers and two trucks in the first ten miles. I had to weave the truck around dozens of mortar rounds sticking up in the road's surface. Dead NVA on both sides of the road. It's hard to link it all in sequence but things had changed. I stayed (in Dak To) until the day after Thanksgiving. The 4th Division fed us turkey next to the airstrip with burning aircraft 100 yards away. The shooting never stopped the whole time."

"We were dug in between two 155 SP's (Self-Propelled Howitzers) just yards on each side. First night I learned to wake up when the hydraulics started to whine. That meant they were ranging and getting ready to fire. I got lump on my head like a golf ball that first shot from hitting the axle of the VHF/crypto trailer I was under."

"A lot of other scary shit happened like my first ground attack but I won't go into it now. I'm shaking a bit now. It changed me. Two days after Thanksgiving, I think, we got out of there. I don't remember who was driving with me that day, but it was pedal to the floor on the horrid road for the whole 26 miles. It never felt so good to be back in my rack that night, that is until about 2:30 am. I had had guard till then and I reported metallic noise in field to our North close by. MACV said the ARVN were out there about 400 meters."

"I was hitting REM sleep when I heard the rounds sliding down the mortar tubes. We were sleeping on the top floor of the just completed barracks with tin roof. One, two, three right down the peak of the roof. The third one made a two- foot hole over my bunk and tail fin went through my bunk and stuck in the floor."

"I was half-way out the door with my M3 grease gun but it (the blast) tore me up and I landed at the bottom of the stairs. Still don't know how. There was an E5 Brasher I think in the water tower and it was his last night before DEROS. He was just burning up the M60 at something 100 yards outside the wire. I climbed on top of the shelter next to the barracks and could see the muzzle flashes of the mortar next to a pile of logs and I dumped both of the .45 magazines I had at the spot before getting down into the bunker."

"My right leg wasn't working by then and when the Lieutenant hiding in there shined a flashlight on me, I shit my pants. I was in my shorts and t shirt and I was covered in holes and chunks of skin and muscle missing. In the end it looked a lot worse that it was but so many people were screwed up and the was blood everywhere. Never saw anyone else from the top floor again."

"I turned 21 a few days later in hospital. I have to tell you those guys (VC/NVA) out there didn't miss a shot. They skipped from building to building and even put one in the Captain's shitter for good measure then skipped the soccer field and did the same to MACV. Our XO lost a kidney or liver I heard but can't remember his name. I was told we had 16 WIA that night."

"I returned just before Christmas. Sorry to be so long winded and my hands are shaking now. You see I believed everyone's day was just like mine. My close friends from school were writing to me from in-country and their day was always worse than mine."

DK: *"Back before Christmas? That was a helluva present."*

JM: *"Why did I come back to the company after that? I still don't know. 1st Sgt. Myers told me I was a dumb ass. I'm sure he was right."*

"There is a whole back story of the first 24 hours but it's nothing I want to talk about. But both buddies were gone in the first few hours. I think we had the first eleven Med Evacs. Don't know why I recall that number. I think there were 26 total and more than a few bent coconuts."

"Time has put a lot of rust on these memories but some things are crystal for a few minutes then thankfully pass. I'm no wordsmith and not close to having taken more *lumps than every other swinging Richard. I still feel someone should know about these guys. I wish I had someone else to help me tell you about Leroy Osborn, Richie Gideon, John Downing or John Rodriquez and so many people there…"*

Chapter Ten

"My Girl"
The Temptations
(Written by Smokey Robinson & Ronald White 1964)
[The 2nd most requested song in my repertoirè]

Daily Grind

February 25, 1968, was the next time I wrote to Lynne, a letter in which I commented repeatedly that I was tired and that I had been traveling. Once again, I didn't reveal or even hint where I had been or for what purpose. Yet, without a doubt, it all was related to the attacks we'd just gone through. All of it was mentally and physical exhausting and I still had my "day job" office duties to perform. Nevertheless, I shared none of the details with Lynne. Instead on this date I included a rambling, handwritten love poem, single-spaced on the front and back of 3 full pages of yellow legal tablet paper.

As mentioned previously, my days at HQ often were a combination of several mundane and routine office tasks like typing those letters of "safe arrival in Vietnam," writing news releases about everyday operations or simple "goings-on," upgrades to communications in the Central Highlands, preparing reports that would be sent up the Chain of Command to 21st Signal Group in Nha Trang, and onto 1st Signal Brigade (and ultimately forwarded to DoD). But I also spent countless hours preparing hard news stories and human-interest stories, all the while searching for or organizing fillers to be included in the monthly *The Unicorn*. Some stories I wrote or prepped were sent up the chain. Yet, I recall only ever seeing one article I had written that was actually published in the "*Army Times*" and distributed worldwide in that publication. I hung a copy of that article on the wall of the "new" information office I moved into after our new commander, LTC Motstko, made significant changes to the HHD-HQ building as well as the landscape around the Pleiku compound.

There was a plethora of reports to file in addition to news articles. Some of the more frequent reports I had to compile were accounts of our Civic Action. In one letter to Lynne I mentioned that I had 4 of those reports going out -- all at the same time. Later, in September 1968, after returning from R&R in Hawaii with Lynne, I mentioned that barracks mate, Joe Caserta, our Battalion Legal Clerk, and I were overwhelmed by our work. I normally went to the office at 7:15 am and rarely got out at the end of the day. Most days it was between 7:30 and 9:00 pm when I finally got back to the barracks. I realize I was living and working in a war zone and getting a few breaks each day while guys on the front were on duty 24/7. These were long days, mentally, emotionally, and physically exhausting days that dragged on for weeks for everyone, indeed!

Publishing a unit newspaper with one or two other GIs as writers was a bit of a 3-ring circus. In reality these guys were "stringers" since they each had a fulltime job either at HQ or at other units where they were assigned. My superior was an officer who was the Editor (in the truest sense of the word) who did little writing other than a monthly column. He simply cleared the stories I submitted and proofed the final version of the paper before it went to press. His relative lack of any other involvement in actual publication was clearly demonstrated by our unit not publishing an edition in June. Instead, since I had severely injured my shoulder in a noncombat-related incident, no paper at all was published that month. I wrote and included a "Xin Loi" article in the combined June-July Edition as an apology for missing an edition. (*Xin Loi* is a polite Vietnamese phrase literally meaning "excuse me".)

Understand, the Editor of a paper is the supervisor, not the writer or physical publisher, but the obvious lapse in publishing, finding no one to fill in for me while I was injured, simply fed my ego and reinforced how important (I felt) I was as "Assistant Editor" in holding this entire endeavor together. To top it off, the day after my injury was finally diagnosed, our CO, Lieutenant Colonel Myron Motsko was convinced I simply was a "goldbricker" trying to get out of doing anything. I truly believe he had no clue about what I did…just a dozen or so steps down the hall from his office.

Conversely, our previous CO, LTC Leo DuBeau, and I spoke frequently and always cordially. He was well aware of my contributions and I of his as CO of our unit. I traveled with him extensively, reporting and photographing his involvement with our troops and with the local Vietnamese in our Civic Action program. On the flip side, I had very few "photo ops" with LTC Motsko (who replaced LTC DuBeau in July) other than taking series of poses for a formal portrait of Motsko sitting at his desk. Glossy 8 x 10 copies of his portrait were printed and distributed to all our units to hang at the entrance to HQ or their Orderly Rooms alongside other members of the Chain of Command up to and including President Lyndon B. Johnson. I simply cannot recall any events, nor do I have any photos of Motsko participating in or attending other types of activities.

Back to publishing the news…our CO wrote a monthly column, several other officers in the unit including our XO, periodically wrote short columns for publication as well. Our Chaplain provided information for a column nearly every month and also provided details about every religious service of every faith scheduled for our Chapel as well as 4th Infantry Division at Camp Enari and the US Air Force at Pleiku Air Base.

Once in a while we included a list of scheduled religious events at other bases, although these were infrequent at best. Ultimately it was up to me and (eventually) SP5 Dick Lytle, a friend and articulate writer who worked in S2, to ferret out stories and write about our units scattered across the Central Highlands. Dick did much of the writing about things coming down from 1st Signal Brigade, 21st Signal Group, and reports out of Washington while I knocked out the stories about the guys in our more remote units, their accomplishments, unit "sports" like volleyball and horseshoe tournaments (yep, those sports) and of course, a fair amount of Civic Action. To do that meant getting to and from those sites to conduct the interviews and gather details about the stories while also holding down my "day job." All of this involved considerable finagling. It meant calling ahead to set up interviews, sometimes starting them over the phone, arranging transportation to and from those sites -- normally by jeep or truck or helicopter, the latter being my favorite and most frequent mode of transportation. At times I would arrange to hitch a ride on whatever aircraft I could -- Army or Air Force, whoever was going my way. I stayed busy in a multitude of ways. I suppose, in a sense and as far as it was possible, I was able to control a tiny part of my journey even though remaining subservient to higher ranks and commands.

Once I had collected info and written the articles for the upcoming edition, I had to do the "budget," a rough layout where I would decide what items might fit on a page, or if lengthy, on what page an article would be continued. I'd then build a typewritten proof around the articles, adding any other PSAs or cartoons that I had been able to get from Army Information Services (AIS). I frequently included my own original line-drawn artwork and cartoons or ones specifically created as unit PSAs. I scrounged or created whatever was needed to fill every space as best I could. Additionally, I hand drew and cut (rather crudely sometimes) the *Nameplate* with two facing unicorns at the top of the first page for each month's edition; they could only be used for one edition because of the fragility of the mimeograph sheets. All of this was finally combined (typed and/or cemented in) on those finicky and fickle mimeograph masters. Typos were a danger to avoid because the mimeo masters were thin, flimsy film that was easily cut or torn. And if that happened, it rendered them useless and I had to begin all over again. Artwork from AIS or elsewhere had to be cemented into a carefully cut space, then a test of those items run, corrections made a final time (hopefully), and a copy of the printed proof given to the Editor for his approval before running the edition. When his approval was granted, SP5 Dave Morales (later SP4 Norm Ackley) printed and collated the 900 copies, stapling the 8½ x 14-inch, back-to-back printed sheets (anywhere from 4 to 10 pages) that made up each month's "edition."

March 1968

I wrote very few notes to Lynne during the month of March. The ones I sent were invariably two-fold in nature. One – constantly bemoaning the long hours spent at my desk and on the road, the latter of which led to being perpetually fatigued. And two, the overall physical conditions of weather and the inordinate stress on my mental health. These, combined with a decreasingly less effective immune system, ultimately led to an on-going struggle against a persistent, nagging cold.

On the "flip side" of communications, I received a personal, unsolicited and curious letter from MACAG-PR in Saigon asking if I might want to transfer. No mention of re-upping or any other contingencies. Their "bait" was limited to the second paragraph:

MACAG-PR   "17 March 1968"

> SUBJECT: Reassignment
>
> "1. Due to DEROS losses, there are a few job openings available to you in the near future."
>
> "2. Working conditions, housing, and recreation facilities are good to excellent, depending on personal tastes." (This contrasted significantly with what we had – none, other than a volleyball court and horseshoe pits in Pleiku.) "Hours are liberal 07:30 to 18:30 daily with 1 ½ hours off for lunch. (and) ... Separate rations are available upon request."
>
> "3. For more information write or call MACV 2571 as soon as possible."
>
> Raymond J. Markiewicz

While I possibly may have known or had some cursory contact with Markiewicz in 1968, as of today I have absolutely no recollection who he was or why he would be extending this offer. (Or why I even saved his unsolicited letter.) I don't think I responded; Saigon was not on my "want to go" list. Yet, I found the offer of a different duty station "with perks" interesting to say the least.

---0---

By now, the rains had begun in earnest. The monsoons brought with them mud, mud, mud, mold, and misery. Yet, there was one encouraging activity I reported on in *The Unicorn* — we got hot showers! Members of Company A built a 3000-gallon water heater for the compound. Now, that was refreshingly good news!

It was good news, but with some always-less-than-good news mixed in. We had no formal laundry to take care of washing our soiled and muddy clothes. Instead, that task was handled by local Vietnamese women who were screened, carded, and searched each time they came into our compound to work. Labor was cheap and it only cost a buck or two a month. But to the Vietnamese whose entire lives and livelihood had been destroyed by the war, being able to work for us was a relief for many of them. Their method of washing was the simple, age-old technique of filling a large shallow pan with cold water, rubbing a bar of soap over the most soiled portion of the garment, then vigorous scrubbing between their hands and repeatedly rinsing and wringing before hanging them to dry on whatever was available. What was available was boxes and crates and barbed wire fence (no clothes pins needed.) They at least did iron our uniforms. Yet, even though most of our clothing was labeled with our names, there was no guarantee you'd get all of your stuff back! Laundry was a mini-conflict of its own.

Likewise, in terms of housekeeping in the barracks, each of us had a young Vietnamese "Mama-San" separate from our laundry Mama-San. She swept and dusted our constantly grimy barracks room and was paid a pittance -- next-to nothing.

I became casual friends with only a few Vietnamese nationals in Pleiku. One in particular was Pham Van Diem, a Vietnamese local who worked at the LAS (NCO) Club. He was one of the few Vietnamese with whom I developed any sort of genuine friendship. So, when I prepared to DEROS back to the states, he gave me a small going away present: a bag of a favorite Vietnamese sesame & peanut crunch candy (kẹo đậu phộng) and gummy fruit candies (mứt), the latter an age-old tradition made for special occasions. His gifts were accompanied by a small notecard with a painting of orchids on the front and a rose on the inside. When fully opened, the card revealed his message scribbled in broken English, albeit much better than my Vietnamese.

"New Year come back to me and yourself too. I wish my friend new year full happiness and I don't forget that I pray with God for friend, full health and hardy to friend can combat V. C. The country Vietnam of me, get Pacific. The flowers in the picture [referring to the illustration on the front and on inside of the card which I still have] *it is very gay. It is not dry and bad. I happy at my friend very much."* Phạm Văn Điêm

His message to me was for happiness. He hoped that the war would end. And he expressed a wish that I might return to visit him in a more peaceful, happy and beautiful Vietnam, not the broken and battered landscape of his beloved city. Unfortunately, his hopes, handwritten on the card I that still keep in a keepsake box on my dresser, would be blotted out entirely an unlucky and unhappy seven years later. I never heard from Van Diem again.

Chapter Eleven

"Baby I Need Your Lovin"
Johnny Rivers
(Written by Holland, Dozier, Holland, Jr 1964)

NCO Clubs and USO Shows
I pick up another "gig" and add another element to this odyssey.

There were dozens of NCO Clubs scattered across Vietnam on every major base and nearly every large Brigade or Battalion size unit plus at many smaller installations. The atmosphere in the clubs was pretty much like local bars back home — at times raucous, lots of drinking, loud conversations, and music playing constantly. Jukeboxes were popular and when coins weren't being fed into them, bartenders at our local LAS Club ("Land Air & Sea" Club in the 43rd Compound) would tune into broadcasts from AFVN Radio-Pleiku (broadcasting from Dragon Mountain near Camp Enari south of the city) or AFVN Radio-Saigon. (AFVN was the acronym for American Forces Vietnam Network.) Once in a while the USO scheduled performers, many Australian, some Asian. These always played to packed clubs.

Of course, the most famous USO program was the Bob Hope Christmas Show. I saw his touring show featuring Raquel Welch and Les Brown's Band shortly after arriving in country, December 26, 1967. It was held at Camp Enari, the 4th Infantry Division Base Camp south of Pleiku. A group of about 25 of us were transported there, packed in the back of a Deuce and a Half. I actually was given an opportunity to go to another show near the end of my Vietnam tour in early December 1968, but I decided to give up my seat for some other guys I felt who deserved it and would enjoy it more than I. After all, I was now very ready to go home in only a week or so.

On a local level, one of the most popular performers at NCO clubs in the Pleiku area was a GI named Lee Dresser who played both guitar and harmonica and had a great singing voice. Lee was with 510th Engineer Company and played regularly at the LAS Club. That's where I met him — and meeting him led to my eventually performing there as well.

From *The Unicorn* February 1968

"LAS Club Offers Variety"

The LAS Club (Land - Air - Sea) of the 43rd Signal Battalion which is located in the A Company Compound area of the Battalion is a surprise package of goodies not often found in other clubs in Vietnam.

The unique feature is not the bar, nor the mixed drinks, nor the snack bar, nor the entertainment, but ALL those things and more. There are slot machines to gobble a few coins on payday, a jukebox on which you can hear some "Oldies but Goodies," and live entertainment throughout each month.

Monday nights are usually reserved for the "Frontiersmen," a local EM rock and roll group that performs just about everything from the Beatles to Beethoven. And there's no denying their popularity. The club is usually filled a half hour before the show begins.

At times the club features talent from outside the Pleiku area. Such performers as "The Dream Boat" and "Cherrise" (sic) have been scheduled in the past. In fact, the young lady mentioned in the previous line played to one of the largest crowds (save Bob Hope's) in the area. And what an entertainer! You'd have to see her variety "show" to believe it. (Even then, you might not.)

Friday nights are the nights that really rock. The club features a "Folk-Rock-Blues" singer by the name of Lee Dresser who has the house "blowing its mind" before he's even halfway through his two and a half hour show. Lee does everything from Bob Dylan to the Stone Ponies to the Temptations and MORE and MORE and MORE and MORE. Superlatives cannot be found to describe the dynamic young singer, Lee Dresser.

For those interested in nourishing themselves with a bit of "good ole USA type" snacks, the LAS Snack Bar offers just about everything from hot dogs and hamburgers to grilled cheese and french fries.

And of course there's always the bar itself. How about a Rum and Coke, Bloody Mary, Seven and Seven, or Screwdriver, or maybe just a plain old Bud or Schlitz or Falstaff? No matter what your taste may be, Scotch, Bourbon, or brew, the LAS probably has it.

The next time you're in the area, stop by. You'll enjoy it and you'll be helping to support those guys who spend the long hours behind the bar, anxious to serve you at all times.

---0---

Besides cold beer or hard liquor at the LAS Club, I personally liked the really thick, juicy and delicious hamburgers served on locally baked artisan Brioche or Kaiser buns—whichever was available. The fries were pretty good as well but had a bit of an odd or "off" flavor, likely from the oil they used over and over. But I felt the food generally beat mess hall chow.

On many days the only meal I ate in the mess hall (if I ate there at all) was breakfast. That was the one meal that was consistent. Eggs, sometimes powdered, sometimes fresh, were normally just scrambled. But if the cooks weren't rushed, they would cook fresh eggs to order. The other breakfast item I looked forward to, but one disdained by many soldiers, was SOS made with ground beef. I tried to never miss that item when it was on the menu. To me all the other meals were pretty plain and, to be frank, I simply didn't care for Army chow, so I didn't eat there with any regularity. There were even times for lunch that I preferred eating some old C Rations at my desk. "C-rats," as they were called by some, were not issued officially to us but I had my own supply line, a temporary barracks-mate who introduced them to me.

That "temporary" roommate was Private George Kondor. He was the "scrounger" for our company. If you wanted it or needed it, George could get it for you. He was sly, slippery, and a masterful con artist. Oddly enough, while he was pretty indifferent to most people, he always treated me very respectfully. He even offered to get me anything I wanted - anything from snacks to a Montagnard Crossbow to an M1 Carbine to ... "whatever." *"Really man, if you want it, I can get it for you."*

I was not in the "market" so to speak for an M1; I had been issued an M14 rifle for use while on duty at the 43rd compound. But if I was on assignment to another unit or a different location, I carried just a standard issue 45 caliber pistol. I've read some of the declassified reports recently and found out that the 43rd did not issue M16s to everyone until the year after I departed. So, only Specialist Dave Clemens, the Colonel's driver, carried an M16 while I was there.

Kondor would barter and trade with all the units in the area for food, booze, weapons, building supplies, you name it. And he did it with US, Korean troops (ROKs), and the Vietnamese - both military *and* civilian (which, as you might guess, was illegal). As far as I know, he likely was a player in the black market in Pleiku scrounging for us as well as the 4th Infantry Division and all the other units in our area. If you needed building materials, or odds and ends of supplies not available through normal military channels (and that was frequent), George could get them. He helped me procure some supplies for a darkroom I would eventually build. The unfortunate thing about George was that he had no respect for military life or military authority, so he was always getting busted. Yet, the last time I saw him, after he had gone AWOL again, he stopped in to see me in our barracks. He was wearing an MP armband and helmet with Military Police insignia on it. I've not been able to find his name listed on the unit roster for either B Company, 504th "Road Runners" who were based at Camp Schmidt just up the road from us or for the 4th Infantry Division MPs at Camp Enari with whom George and I both had numerous contacts. Thus, it very well may have been another creative and evasive ruse of his. I'll never know. It's just another twisted element of this sojourn … and it doesn't really matter.

Chapter Twelve

"What's Your Name?"
Don & Juan
(Written by Claude Johnson - 1962)

April 1968

At one point during my tour, someone "further up the Chain of Command"— either Army Information Services (AIS) or, more likely, someone in 1st Signal Brigade IO asked me to begin a series of radio interviews focusing on the "unsung" members of our units, most notably GIs working in our more remote units. I sent these tape recordings to 1st Signal Brigade in Saigon. They forwarded them to a facility in either Saint Louis or Kansas City for processing and distribution. After clearing a security review, they were sent to the hometown radio stations of the soldiers I interviewed. I don't recall how many of these interviews I did, but the job took me to a few sites that were much more insecure than my home base in Pleiku. This turned out to be a very time consuming process involving finding guys willing to be interviewed, clearing it with their CO, scheduling transportation to the unit (generally by jeep in and around Pleiku, but more often by helicopter to other sites), finding a time that the interview would not interfere with the GI's job, trying to avoid too much background noise –everything from helicopters to artillery -- and actually getting the guys to "open up." There were times I free-styled or "doubled up" on interviews. That is, I flew or caught a ride to a unit to do a written story of some sort, then tried to convince one of our guys there also to grant a radio interview.

There's no doubt it was an ego boost to hear myself on the radio, "This is Army Specialist Dennis Kaltreider reporting from Kontum" (or Cheo Reo or whatever site I was broadcasting from in the Central Highlands of Vietnam.) But it was a frustrating "vain-gain" at best. Eventually it took too much time while trying to complete all the other elements of my job. I think I conducted less than a dozen of these radio assignments over the period of several months.

I did conduct interviews in Kontum, (located about an hour north of Pleiku), Ban Me Thuot (located about 4 hours due south of Pleiku in Dak Lak Province), Cheo Reo, located half way between Pleiku and Ban Me Thuot and slightly east of those two cities, and An Khe, east of Pleiku and not far from Qui Nhon and the South China Sea.

One of the "critical" sites I visited was Dak To. It was critical insofar as it sat in the "tri-border" area where the borders of Vietnam, Cambodia, and Laos meet and was near a main branch of the Ho Chi Minh Trail aka in Vietnamese as *Đuong Truong Son,* and sometimes called "The Blood Road" due to the incessant US bombing of it. Virtually everything the VC and NVA forces needed to fight in the south, from weapons, vehicles, food and medical supplies, to medical personnel and combat troops (up to 20,000 a month) were moved along this trail! Most individuals moved down the trail primarily on foot. It could take an individual as many as six months to make the grueling trip traversing mountains, streams and rivers, and slogging through thick rainforests where the trail was cut. Materials and supplies were transported via everything imaginable: carts, wagons, trucks, jeeps, tanks, bicycles, and even carried in backpacks and shoulder-slung baskets. The trail was used constantly, in every kind of weather, day and night. Nighttime trekkers were said to have used lightning bugs inside small rice paper lanterns hanging from their backpacks to help follow each other on the ofttimes treacherous trail.

The North Vietnamese were incredibly resourceful and excavated the trail almost exclusively by hand with intricate interconnecting tunnels and concealed entrances to hide trail travelers when US planes flew over to bomb or for travelers to rest. Radio and telecommunications facilities, food and weapons caches, medical aid stations and barracks, all were concealed underground.

Our small base at Dak To was originally set up to support 4th Infantry Division and elements of the 503rd Airborne and 173rd Airborne's Operation McArthur from November 3 to November 23, 1967. That action resulted in some of the bloodiest battles of the war and the area remained part of a critical, ongoing "border" defense. This effort was planned to stem the rising concentration and infiltration of enemy forces to the West and South of the area. Although Top Secret and completely denied at that time, Dak To was being (and continued to be) used as a Forward Operations Base for MACV-SOG covert-black ops.

First Signal Brigade's "official" involvement ended when Dak To was deactivated in early 1968. However, I've been told firsthand by members of 1st Signal Brigade who were there -- that we maintained some presence and involvement in that area long after our "official" involvement ended.

I was sent to Dak To, **April 8-9, 1968**, to accompany 1st Signal Brigade Commander Brigadier General VanHarlingen, Jr. who was carrying out an inspection of the stand-down. (All my photos from that trip went directly to Brigade Headquarters, so I have none to share other than the aerial photos of the camp I took from our Huey. I've included one of these in the Appendix.)

By **April 22, 1968**, attacks on our compound in Pleiku had slowed significantly, save for very random harassment mortars hitting us at night or, more often shelling the nearby airbase. The NVA Mini-Tet May Offensive wouldn't come for another several weeks. As a result of this more relaxed atmosphere, I began to enjoy a little more off duty time. Inasmuch as I am constantly active (restless) and not one to sit by idly doing little more than drinking, I restarted my "music performances avocation" that had begun in Fredy's Jazz Club in Bogotá, Colombia, and continued in other private venues around Bogotá and Medellín. I described my re-entry into the music scene via a letter I wrote to Lynne the following day.

April 23, 1968

"I think I've found the answer. Last night a group that was to play at the [LAS] *club didn't show up - three of their members came down with food poisoning - so I hurriedly scrounged a guitar and amp and speakers and microphone - not the best - but acceptable (under the circumstances) and decided to play for about an hour."*

"It wasn't good - I wasn't well prepared - my fingers cramped from lack of playing - I didn't have a full "show" lined up. However, I played! - - - - -"

"The club was packed even though it was pouring down rain and a lot of guys had come a fair distance to see the show [that had been scheduled]. *I played from about 8:20 - after much trouble with our rain-soaked equipment - until 9, took a 5-minute break, played another hour until 10, took another 3 minute break, and went on until about 10:35. The club was supposed to close at 10:15 but they let me and the 70-odd "followers" remain a while longer - and even then, perspiring, hoarse, exhausted...they didn't want me to leave the stage."*

"Perhaps with a bit more practice, I'll be able to really throw a show for the guys."

Well, I did practice, and I did more shows. I have no idea how many except when I wrote to Lynne sometime later, I commented that I was performing several nights a week at different NCO Clubs in the area and it was beginning to become rather grueling. After all, I still had a day job. Nonetheless, I guess the practice paid off—even better than I expected and in more than one way. These gigs gave me something constructive to do as well as a bit of "pin money," usually 50 bucks a night. That was a significant sum for just a night's performance at that time. And it was usually accompanied by a free drink or two.

Without a doubt, Lee Dresser was the most versatile and crowd-pleasing favorite performer in our area. My personal style was quite different from his at the outset. I patterned my early performances in a style similar to one I followed that was highly popular with Peace Corps

Volunteers in Colombia. My sets included folk songs, a handful of country tunes, and quite a few 1950s Rock and Roll songs. Blues were part of Lee's shows but a very insignificant part of mine. But, little by little I tried to modify my shows for this very different audience by adding more contemporary 1960s rock which the guys (and gals - Nurses and Donut Dollies) were requesting. My sets were a mix of all those genres and slowly falling a bit more in line with the tunes that we were hearing on AFVN.

Side note: Just prior to leaving for Vietnam, I was interviewed by a newspaper in York, PA. The article also featured an up-and-coming local disc-jockey, Sue Wolf who actually conducted the interview. She quoted/labelled my music, writing, and performing style as, "Folk-Pop." In Vietnam it was much more a mishmash of that with a hard Rock and Roll twist.

May 2, 1968

"I got the Eugene McCarthy campaign button you sent .... put it in my footlocker; don't flash it around much...not the "prevailing attitude at HQ."

---0---

Al Dawson was an Information Specialist with 1st Signal Brigade in Saigon. We had met earlier in the year, likely right after Tet when he was doing follow-up reports about the incredible job our units were doing in the field. In addition to his work as a journalist, Al was the contact individual and conduit for the "hometown" radio interviews I did of our guys. (Incidentally, the radio interview that Al conducted with me was sent to my hometown stations, WNOW, WORK, and WSBA in York, PA. However, Lynne does not remember hearing it broadcast.) As a part of the interview, Al asked me to describe my work with our units scattered across the Central Highlands, and especially the Civic Action work we were performing. Off air, he and I discussed ways that I could arrange to provide additional support for Dr. Pat Smith's Hospital in Kontum.

"Dr. Pat" as she was called by just about everyone, was a dedicated humanitarian from Seattle who moved to Vietnam in the 1950s and established the Minh Quy Hospital (aka Catholic Mission Hospital). Her heartfelt goal was to provide care for Montagnard tribespeople near Kontum.

Members of C Company, 43rd Signal Battalion often helped her by doing repairs and donating money and supplies to support her efforts. Throughout the year our men also gave toys to the children in the Montagnard Villages nearby. It was reported that some entire Montagnard families travelled on foot nearly 60 miles just to get treatment at the hospital. Dr. Pat worked at her clinic-hospital and safe haven for the vulnerable and underserved Montagnards, administering aid and treatment for nearly 15 years, 1960 to 1975. During the Tet Offensive her hospital was attacked and overrun. The Viet Cong raided her hospital, threw hand grenades and shot up the lab with the intention of kidnapping her. Fortunately, they were unable to do so because she happened to be in the city of Kontum during the attack. (One report said she was hidden under a "pile" of her patients who were shielding her. Regardless, she evaded capture.) However, the Viet Cong did kidnap one of her staff, a German nurse named Renata Kuhnen. The enemy also took at least one of her Montagnard patients. Several members of C Company volunteered to accompany a Special Forces Unit on a mission to rescue the nurse and patient. Sadly, they were unsuccessful.

However, Renata's story doesn't end there. Happily, a year after her kidnapping, her captors released her and she was escorted back to Kontum by a group of Montagnards.

May 2, 1968

>*Denny, Just got a minute to bang this out to you before guard duty starts. Called my friends at CBS and NBC on Pat Smith and both sounded most interested. Probably they will drop up real soon.*
>
>*Cy Wolen at CBS is wearing dual hats these days, and this is the purpose of the letter. He is operations manager or some such for a group called AIM— something like American International Medicine or.....(a good reporter takes exact notes, right?) Anyhow he is very interested in what Pat might like to have in the way of supplies...*
>
>*Anyhow he says to tell Dr. Smith to write to him at the below address and tell him just what she needs. He says right now they're dying to give stuff away to Americans because when they give them to Viets, they steal and sell them (on the black market). So pls (sic) get word to her....*
>
>*Pardon the typing. I'm typing with sunglasses on because of a gd infected eye I picked up. 40 days and countin' down, E.T.S.*
>
>*Love, Al Dawson*

Al included 2 where I could contact CBS: Room 206, Caravelle Hotel, Saigon, and the other at CBS News, JUSPAO, APO.

Update: He did not return to the US, but rather, continued his career in journalism and went on to become UPI Bureau Chief in Saigon. He remained through the fall of Saigon in 1975. From Saigon he moved to Thailand, was expelled from there in 1984, then later was allowed to return. He gained international recognition as a journalist and author.

As of March 2019, he was still writing an op-ed column for the Bangkok Post.

Unfortunately, I do not know the ultimate outcome of my efforts to provide assistance to Dr. Pat. CBS did air a documentary on her as part of their "Twentieth Century" TV series hosted by Walter Cronkite. Dr. Pat stayed in Kontum until she was forced to abandon her hospital in 1975. When she fled, she took along her two adopted Montagnard sons, Det and Wir and returned to the United States. She died December 26, 2004 in Olympia, WA. May this wonderful *Angel of the Highlands* rest in eternal peace.

May 3, 1968

"It didn't rain as much today as yesterday and the hours before - the nights are still damp - the dry season is far off - yet a glimmer of warmth is noted .... much bickering, arguing, stalling - tho it is a start. It is 10:32 pm - we just heard the preliminary talks will begin the 10th - perhaps, just perhaps, someday not too far distant there will be some semblance of peace in our wounded Earth." [This was the perpetual hope and prayer of virtually every GI in Vietnam.]

And then a significant, sad, and somber day blackened my calendar.

May 5, 1968

"Dear Lynne,

Today a convoy got hit between here and Kontum - 3 of our people got killed, and one was a very, very good friend...it's all so terrible.... understand love .... Please ... no matter what ... I do love you and shall forever."

I was shaken by this tragic incident and for years I steadfastly blocked it from my memory, just as I apparently have done with details of a number of other incidents. Until now, I consciously chose not to ever mention it to anyone, never discussed it, and I never wrote about it except to Lynne. It was one of several troubling and onerous times during my tour I did not want to recall.

But now, over 50 years later, perhaps I can begin to ease some of the guilt and anguish I have felt if I begin to talk about it. Yet, even if I do, I know that the sadness of this event will never ever go away.

In the course of outlining and writing this book, I hesitantly began to mentally reconstruct this specific incident. I read a letter I wrote to Lynne the day after the incident. I also reread the articles that I wrote for *The Unicorn* in May 1968, copies of which I had kept packed away in unopened boxes for nearly half a century. During the immediate past year (2019), I corresponded with my friend, "Monterey Jack" Mahan who was mentioned earlier in the article about C Company's valiant defense of their compound during the first days of Tet. He shared personal information about this ambush, the friends we both lost, and the grim aftermath of dealing with the damaged trucks, the details of which are simply too horrific to include here. For me, all the rest is simply a fuzzy obscure hole in my memory.

One day earlier…May 4, 1968 - A Sad Day

The details, as best I recall: It was now several months after the Tet Offensive. On Saturday night, May 4, 1968, I played one of my music gigs at our LAS Club in the 43rd Compound. One of the guys in attendance was a friend, Donnie Campbell, a GI from Detroit. Donnie came to the club on numerous occasions when I was performing, and he was always very supportive. We became good friends; we were close to the same age; Donnie was 3 months younger than me. We shared some other common bonds as well but mostly we talked about the music I played…and the style of music being heard more and more on AFVN Radio, most notably thanks to Adrian Cronauer's iconoclastic broadcasts.

During a break on Saturday night we were chatting and I mentioned that I was flying to Kontum on Monday, May 6th. Donnie said, "I'm driving up there tomorrow (Sunday). Wanna ride along?" Donnie was a "Heavy Vehicle Driver," an oxymoron for this slight-built young man. He was based in Qui Nhon but regularly stopped in at the 43rd LAS Club in Pleiku before continuing with his transport of materials, equipment, and supplies up Highway 14 to Kontum. I gave his offer a passing thought, figuring I could work out the details, but I knew that I still had some responsibilities at HQ and our CO always wanted me by his side to take notes — and especially-always for the more than obvious photo ops. So, ultimately, I declined his offer to ride shotgun with him and said that I'd check in with him Monday when I landed in Kontum.

Late the next day, Sunday afternoon, May 5, a friend called from our motor pool asked if I had heard about Donnie's convoy. "No," I said, I hadn't. That's when he said, "Oh" and paused. "The convoy got ambushed. They just towed Donnie's truck in and it's bad."

Puzzled by the call, Frank Swegheimer and I walked over to the motor pool, which was located beyond the Personnel Office, and as I approached, I knew almost at once I really didn't want to be there. This was going to be decidedly unpleasant.

In a phone call (2019), Frank told me he clearly remembers the Motor Pool Sergeant strongly cautioning us, "Don't touch a thing!" But it was an unnecessary admonition.

The convoy, along with Donnie's truck and several others, had been ambushed by a Battalion from the 32nd Regiment of the North

Vietnamese Army just outside of Kontum. The cab of Donnie's truck was riddled with bullet and small arms holes and perhaps an RPG. Donnie never made it to Kontum. He died outright just 2 months short of going home. The vision of that severely damaged and blood-stained truck still brings a sickening lump to my throat.

Had I accepted Donnie's offer to ride along with him, it's certain I never would have made it home and this account would never have been written.

Rest in peace, dear friend. Rest in peace....SP4 Donald A. Campbell, 64th Trans Co, 124th Trans Btn, 8th Trans Gp, Qui Nhon, 1st Logistics Command.

At least nine other US soldiers were KIA and 16 listed as WIA in that ambush. Three of the nine killed were members of the 43rd.

--PFC John Leslie Downing was from Phoenix, AZ, who worked in supply and was assigned to C Company, Kontum.

--Sp 4 Harold Thomas Henesy, from Saint Petersburg, FL, was a Multichannel Systems Operator, assigned to C Company, Kontum.

--PFC Larry D. Williams was from Minneapolis, MN. He was a truck driver based at my home unit HHD 43rd Signal Battalion, Pleiku.

I didn't personally know these other guys from our unit. Nor did I know any of the other men killed in this ambush. Nevertheless, I carry a heavy burden in my heart; I mourn unabashedly. And I am truly saddened by their loss.

On Monday, **May 6, 1968**, I flew to Kontum with our CO as planned, albeit under a pall of gut-wrenching sadness and the reality of being one of the luckiest sons'o bitches in the world.

And I will always, always wonder, why?

---0---

In September 1986, I visited the Vietnam Memorial Wall in Washington, DC, for the very first time. I was in the capital city attending a National Conference to commemorate the 25th Anniversary of the Peace Corps. Several of my fellow Colombia Volunteers with whom I had worked in 1964-1966 invited me to visit the memorial with them. I hesitantly agreed, but when we got there, I could not bring myself to look at the wall or read any of the names on it. I simply walked the length of it alongside my friends, completely averting my eyes both times we passed by it. I knew whose names were inscribed there. But I simply could not bear to look and read them. I hope they forgive me.

Years later I visited the wall again. But this time I looked and saw and touched the wall, sorrowful tears flooding my eyes and obscuring my vision.

And now, after exhaustive reflection, I think I've come to the realization that perhaps one of the many reasons I've been haunted by the event of May 5th, 1968, ... as much, if not more so than any other during my tour of Vietnam ... and perhaps part of why I have struggled to write this account even now ... is that I feel an unmitigated, lasting guilt and ... I never got to say, "Goodbye," to my friend. I have not found closure. And I am convinced I never will.

----0----

May 11, 1968

"It is noon, hot and shimmering, a blue day of skies with only a few winks of clouds.

"Strange — no, beautiful — for the past few days there have been butterflies in impressive numbers glazing each day. I first saw them one morning after the mist had all but disappeared. We looked and batted an eyelash and they appeared...yellow and while, some even dark like a dark blue or darker. more than I'd e're seen before. Amazing...
"

It's very likely these "swarms," sometimes called "kaleidoscopes" of butterflies were the Orange Oakleaf Butterfly that was mimicked (in some ways) by the Viet Cong. The butterflies would take flight as necessary and then, when endangered, drop to the ground, close their wings so their bright colors would be hidden and only plain brown was showing. They would remain there totally still, perfectly resembling a dead leaf. What masterful camouflage!

May 13, 1968

For some of my music gigs I began teaming up with another GI from A Company named David Page Alderman (aka "Groovy") .... Dave was a good guitarist, our voices blended well, and he had an electronic drum kit that added a lively, entirely new dimension and broader, more complete sound to our performances.

"We played at the Air Force last night....Dave broke a string, the electronic drum set went on the blink, a screw fell out of my guitar" [it held the electric pick-up in place] *"then I broke a string — finally we went to work and laid 'em out on the last set."*

"I ran into a guy by the name of Eme who was in A-7-2 [our Personnel AIT group] *at Knox. He was sent to the 101st Airborne as a clerk - they gave him a gun. He's been up to Dak To and the A Shau Valley - came down with some*

of his buddies and were guests of the Air Force last night. They liked the show so much they made us "honorary" members of Company C, 101st Airborne and gave us Screaming Eagles patches and parachutist badges — I felt like Bob Hope .... for a minute."

Unfortunately, Dave smoked too much weed, and eventually began acting kind'a crazy. One day, with no hint, or warning, or confiding in me about any of his problems, he simply stripped buck naked, calmly walked out of our compound and over the hill to the Evac Hospital. I never saw him again.

I returned to my solo performances — while he was sent to a hospital in Japan, eventually discharged, then apparently sent home.

May 17, 1968

On this day, my note to Lynne was written on a handful of small, pocket-size sheets from my reporter's notepad.

"It's 12:45 pm and I'm sitting at Camp Enari, the 4th Infantry Division Base in Pleiku, waiting here for the arrival of Col. McElwee, the Commander of the 21st Signal Group. I have the 'pleasure' of driving his sedan today. Apparently, I am the only person at HHD "qualified" with US Army 348 .... licensed as a limo driver!"

I suppose the army thought that if I could drive a Main Battle Tank, I could drive a limo. Sigh!

May 19, 1968

An Unusual Assignment for a Rather Extended Strange Day

"Good morning, love. It's now 00:15 or 12:15 am. Yesterday I had the exquisite pleasure (you've got to be kidding) of having headcount — that means that I kept a record of persons eating in our mess hall — wow! I'm glad to say I won't have to pull it again. I had to be here at 5 am yesterday — until 7:15 am. Then from 11:30 am to 6 pm I had the same (lousy) job. And, of course, here I am this morning — if you're wondering what I'm doing here at this crazy hour — we have a midnite meal for our shift workers."

"I shouldn't complain about today — it did get me out of the office for the afternoon and, in addition to my regular task of counting heads (with bodies attached) I monitored the suds. That is, we had free beer for the members of our company — A Company had theirs too."

"Let's start back a bit. Normally chow hours are not all afternoon. However, today we had a cookout — that's why the long hours and free beer. Anyhow, I was instructed to insure (sic) that our guys had a beer or soda to partake with their steak — naturally."

"Since it was sunny, brite, etc. I had a beer or two myself — would you believe 15 to be almost exact?!? Oh, well, I'll keep my eyes closed so as to not bleed to death. It's just about quitting time."

It seems the cookout — a complete surprise and the only time steak was ever served — was indeed, a rarity and set up in honor of Col McElwee's visit. However, the absolute worst part of the entire "event" was that the fires to cook the steaks were doused with kerosene or diesel to get the locally-made charcoal – purchased in downtown Pleiku -- started. That completely destroyed the flavor. I took a bite or two out of mine, threw it away, and grabbed another beer. My only memento from that debacle is a photo of the charcoal dealer in downtown Pleiku.

May 24, 1968

"Intelligence radio communications warned us we were going to get nailed last night — but we didn't. Seems they never really know." ..... "Civic Action report due tomorrow. Have much to do." [This is the first time I have found any reference of any sort to security or intelligence in my hundreds of letters to Lynne.]

May 25, 1968

"It's 6:45 am and I've got 4 reports to compile and submit today (Civic Action). Of course, I'm working feverishly on the paper. And now, instead of one telephone on my desk I have three for me: Pleiku # 3732, 3641, 3643 plus HHD, Adjutant 3741 .... Oh, and Frank's number is Pleiku 3841."

During May 1968 we had a significant turnover in personnel - especially at the top. Some of that change is reflected in one of the many letters I wrote during the month. Even though our comm guys were doing an amazing and vital job keeping communications open all the time, HQ was beginning to resemble some of the goofiness portrayed many years later in the book and movie M*A*S*H.

May 27, 1968

"Dearest Love — I am tired tonite—tired in body, spirit, and all...I am in a bad mood tonite. Sorry..."

"Normally we work from 7:30 am to 5 pm. However, lately we've been pulling details for at least an additional hour to an hour and a half — sometimes 7:15 am -7:30 pm. Needless to say, I believe it might be necessary. BUT we do not improve our perimeter defenses. We do not repair our bunkers. We do not work on the things that might possibly be the difference between losing our lives or allowing us to survive. Well, what in the HELL are we doing?. We are "beautifying" the area. We are planting grass...and we have made flower gardens ....."

"We have a 275 actually (probably over 300) pound Sergeant Major who just arrived from the states, The group commander (also) just arrived from the states. They DO NOT know there is a god-damned war going on in this fucking place. They are back in their own damn dream world..."

"Oh, but that's not all—we're looking for a flag pole, records of march music and bugle calls so that every day we can stand outside in formation and play "the old time soldier"—"it's tradition"...BULL..."

"Hon...forgive me, but it's impossible to even try to think about this mess with any sense of comprehension...A guy dies — is murdered by the Viet Cong or NVA; they blow taps and say, "fuck it.""

"PS...Mail is bad......no one's getting any....Damn this place..."

May 29, 1968

"Today for a change there was mail...13 pieces ...... I got #84 thru 88 (minus 87) from thee...I LOVE THEE SO VERY VERY MUCH!" And I got the strings for my guitar in the 6th letter....Well, it's time to print the paper and we have NO paper to print it...so I'm trying to scrounge some."

May 30, 1968

"It's 6:20 pm on the 30th of May...got letter #87 (the lost one) yesterday. I (also) got #78 yesterday! Like I said the other nite, mail is really messed up."

"I got the paper typed up today so it could go out early...but — no paper for the paper. So I scrounged some from the 4th Infantry Division. So then what? The mimeo broke down. Luckily, it's operable again. So I guess we'll 'put the paper to bed' tonight. BUT I know something I'd rather put to bed....namely YOU, Mrs. Kaltreider. I am ready to explode!"

"One hundred and five days to R&R. One hundred and ninety-eight to total BLISS with thee, with me, with US TOGETHER."

June 9, 1968

The men of HHD and Company A built a new chapel in the 43rd Compound spearheaded by Cpt Tomas Denson, a man I truly admired. I helped a few times, pounded a few nails during the construction, took photos, and attended services there on a number of Sundays. Cpt Denson was replaced by Major John Edgar just three days after the chapel was completed. A lot more staff changes continued to take place during this month, not only in our headquarters unit, but at higher levels within 1st Signal Brigade and 21st Signal Group. While enlisted men generally remained with the same unit for the duration of their tour, some Senior NCOs and Officers were replaced about every six months. And special-skilled communication operators might be transferred on a "as needed basis" or TDY (Temporary Duty) to units that lost members to KIA, WIA, or DEROS or for whatever reason. But generally speaking, officers were reassigned more frequently than enlisted.

June 19, 1968

"AM terribly afraid this is going to be very short…..we have IG inspection coming up next week and things here are really messed up. It seems as if everyone around here has forgotten that there is a war going on around us. We have rifle inspections and all kinds of bull every morning, details every night and we work in our offices the rest of the time. Thank you for reading Meg's letter to me [on a tape-recording Lynne sent to me] *…it was nice!!! Haven't seen or heard from John for a while. I really do hope that things work out for Meg and John."* (I'm happy to report they did, in fact, get married after the war and are still together as of the writing of this book.)

IG Inspection was a BIG deal. Everything absolutely had to be spic & span, ship-shape, "STRAC" in Army terms. And even more than we did after rocket and mortar attacks, we now had to "police" the compound. That meant walking through the entire HHD and Company A areas elbow to elbow, "finger tip to finger tip," picking up every piece of shrapnel and debris from the attack down to the smallest metal fragment. It was back breaking in a sense and a few of us would take turns alternating bending over to pick up pieces that were near us. This debris, often sharp shards of metal from the enemy rounds and sometimes larger chunks of steel, was deposited in empty food cans from the Mess Hall.

June 20, 1968

"Once again, the peaceful-cool morning has greeted me with gray skies and I sit with only a few seconds in which to tell thee of all the love and trust and want and need and missing in my heart so far from thee."

June 23, 1968

"…have pretended to ignore the problems at hand by playing volleyball and even sleeping!"

"Oh, Hon, I'm so exhausted—so tired of this whole mess…..Today can I just be weak for a second and turn to thee for help?….." *"Am thinking about dropping out of the singing circuit…it's getting to be too much of a hassle. Plus with the additional money we'll be getting* [because of my promotion to E5] *there's really no need for me to do it…other than to just be in the limelite."*

This note proved to be unintentionally prophetic about events that would transpire the very next day.

Chapter Thirteen

"(I Can't Get No) Satisfaction"
Rolling Stones
(Written by Mick Jagger & Keith Richards - 1965)
[Probably the third most requested song in my performances.]

June 26, 1968

"Dearest: You'll never guess what I did. If you look closely at the photo you'll see my right arm is in a sling. Neat, huh?"

In this letter to Lynne, I had enclosed a photo of me standing in front of my desk with my right arm fully wrapped and hidden in an ominous black sling. It was not a smart thing to do and, even though I was smiling in the photo, and trying to appear light-hearted about the event, my letter and photo nearly scared her to death. What an idiot I was!

"SUMMARY: Playing volleyball, husband chases ball, collides with 245 pound giant, falls, giant continues right over, lands on [my back &] shoulder, pulling it out of socket and possibly tearing some ligaments. Oh well ....."

"I'll write more when I can manipulate these keys with my left hand or tape soon. By the way, that's part of my office in the background. Behind me are the Chain of Command photos."

On the wall "Top left is the "Chicken Switch" or "Red Alert Siren" and the Enemy Activity Report work sheet, then Map of RVN. Above that—Command Bunker Arms Key. My desk —junk, typewriter (on work table) and 3 phones..."

71st Evacuation Hospital – Pleiku

The 71st Evac was just a short distance "over the hill" -- not far from the 43rd compound. I got to know parts of it personally in two distinctly different ways...first as a performer in their Officers Club and now, … as a non-combat-injured outpatient.

As described in the letter to Lynne...I had been playing volleyball with friends in our Battalion Volleyball League the afternoon of June 24 when a very large, husky guy and I both dove for a ball. I landed first and he landed on top of me with his full weight, jamming my shoulder into the hard clay.

I had trouble getting to my feet and when I finally was able to stand up, I found I couldn't move my right arm. It just hung limp by my side and it hurt like hell! I knew something was quite wrong and I needed to get it checked. Someone brought a jeep up from the motor pool and drove me to the hospital that was located about a half mile away.

As I noted, the Evac Hospital was busy nearly all the time treating wounded and injured soldiers from all over the Central Highlands. The day I showed up at the 71st was no exception.

June 27, 1968

"I was x-rayed the evening of the 24th about a half-hour after it happened. They (the doctor examining the x-rays) said that I had no fracture nor dislocation, but just a "slight" bruise. So they bound me up in a sling and said, "Out into the cold, cold world…"

"But it's been bothering me for a few days, so I went to the dispensary yesterday morning. Between 8:45 and 9:30 I waited for doctor to look at it. He, after a small consultation, decided it should be re-x-rayed. So between 9:45 and 10:15 I waited in the emergency ward of the 71st Evac Hospital again. They took 4 shots of it and told me to wait. Along comes 11:30 and they decide they need more x-rays! Finally, at 12:05 they tell me to go back to the dispensary … where they told me to go back to the orthopedic clinic because my doctor wouldn't be in and he wouldn't be able to help me anyway. … So, back to the hospital."

"So, I hand my records to the clerk, who in turn hands them back to me and says, "Oh, no you don't. Come back tomorrow at 0900."

"So now it's the afternoon of tomorrow and I'm telling thee that I went back this morning and went to another doctor who said, "Geez, you must have broken a collarbone." And I said, "Ouch!" and he said, "Let's look at your x-rays. Hmm. Say, Lefty, you've got a sprained AC joint." And I said, "What's that?" And he says, "Well, it isn't sprained too bad; it's just a good ole painful shoulder separation, like your collarbone's been done knocked out of whack and it ain't sittin' in the socket like it ought to be. Or, as they say out west, 'it's dislocated and discombobulated."

Finally! A doctor with a sense of humor. But I was in too much pain to truly appreciate his kind-hearted humor. Considering what these doctors and nurses went through everyday…. well, God Bless Them!

"He then said, 'It's about a half or three-quarters inch out of place'."

"So after people telling me it's "only a bruise" and to stop gold-bricking …. it's not! I've got to wear the sling another week — then 6 days of heat and Physical Therapy. And then another week of waiting, then more x-rays and PT every 3 days for a few more weeks. But it's probably only bruised! Ha!"

Our relatively new CO, LTC Motsko, who arrived from the Armed Forces Staff College in Norfolk, VA, a week after my injury, was not convinced I had actually suffered an injury. He rather angrily said, "You still have one good arm, so you can just come into the office and answer the damn phone!" So, I did…one handed.

In the end, I got to meet some really great, caring medical personnel along with a few other staff members at the 71st Officers Club, especially during my music gigs. Funny happenstance…the director of the 71st Evac Club was not aware that I had been injured. A few days, perhaps less than a week after my injury, he phoned me at the Information Office and asked if I could do a show Saturday night at the club. When I described to him what happened, he still didn't seem to understand and remained almost insistent. He continued to beg me to perform. But that wasn't going to happen since my arm was still in a sling and I had no other way to accompany myself. On top of that, they still hadn't paid me the $50 from my last gig. They had a habit of paying when I showed up for the next gig rather than right after the show itself. But, little did I know that the performance prior to my injury was indeed, my last gig there … and I never did get paid!

July 2, 1968

Prayers and Candles at Home

I attended church irregularly. However, at the same time worship services were being held in Pleiku each Sunday morning (9:30-10:30 am, Indochina Time), Lynne and my mother each lit a special candle at their homes in PA. They lighted those two red pillar candles during the corresponding hour (9:30-10:30 pm Eastern Time, Saturday evening in PA) each week for the entire year I was gone, knowing that I was thinking about and likely praying for them at virtually the very same time. (Lynne brought her candle to Hawaii when we met for R&R, and she and I lighted the candle there, enjoying the symbolism of sharing this tradition together.)

I used everything I could get my hands on to write to Lynne. "Real stationery" was not readily available, unless included in a "care package" sent from home, so the following note was written on the back of a church bulletin from June 30, 1968.

"Dearest Love,

"I will tape tonite—I have Commander of the Relief…it'll finally afford us a bit of time together."

"Through the damp, the rain, the dark, the fear, the feeling of utter helplessness, shines my love for thee. And with this too, a pledge to last until eternity lasts no more, hope is a truth never seen by any man, life in its entirety (sp) fails to

exist in any part of the galaxies...my love, my life, my all is thine, alone, forever and more."

This particular night duty as Commander of the Relief was one I remember very clearly and there are parts of it I can visualize with reasonable clarity. It is one of the times that reinforced my superstition about sending Lynne tapes, because just as I began to record during my time as Commander of the Relief, the howitzers began firing from Artillery Hill. It began to seem like every time I started a recording to Lynne, Charlie would hit us or drop several mortar rounds nearby. I only taped half a tape this night and recounted the event to Lynne in a note the following day.

July 8, 1968

"....again as every three days, I went to the hospital this morning for therapy. Altho improving, it seems to hurt all the time as if there was no healing possible. However, I've been assured by so many people that it will go away within three weeks."

In this letter, typed awkwardly with my left hand, I spoke at length about flying to Hawaii to meet her for R&R in September.

July 16, 1968

Apparently since I was of limited use with my arm in a sling, my superiors thought I could best be used at night for Commander of the Relief. I wrote the following note after pulling another all-night CoR.

"Dearest, I don't know if you know, but I tried to call you (early this morn). I phoned a friend in An Khe who runs the MARS station and he put the call through about 6:30 pm for you. Well, he was going to call back — I waited, and waited, and finally phoned him again only to find out he HAD gotten a call through but when he tried to ring me back, there was no answer. I was furious! Four of our damn phones went out and he said he rang for 3 minutes — solid ringing. This place really gets you down. We're supposed to be a Signal Battalion and we can't even get our own phones to ring."

The MARS station (Military Auxiliary Radio Station) was run by the Department of Defense and had its origins sometime in 1925. The "system" in Vietnam was set up to allow GIs to call home. It used a series of designated military radio operators broadcasting on civilian Single Side-Band radios. A GI would normally visit the MARS Center, request a call and wait for the military operator in Vietnam to "patch through" his call to a civilian, licensed amateur radio operator, an official MARS network operator in the US. That US operator would then place a collect call via telephone to the service member's home. Many times it worked, albeit awkwardly with both calling parties having to pause in their conversation and say, "over" as a cue for the ham operators to switch from transmit to receive and vice versa. But for Lynne and me, MARS was a complete failure. Lynne's phone apparently did ring and the operator told her, "I think someone is trying to call you from Vietnam." But then it broke down on my end when the MARS operator couldn't ring me.

July 23, 1968

"Finished with physical therapy — full movement restored, yet as I said last night in the note on the church bulletin (July 21) it's crikky now and then. And I have a terrible cold! Damn."

July 25

"....been pouring unmercifully for the last two days—perhaps the monsoons have arrived. Drat!"

Due to my late June injury, we missed publishing an edition for that month and chose to publish a "combined" June-July *The Unicorn*, which included a handful of news releases from First Signal Brigade IO and a couple of features or short columns and fillers by other people in the unit including SSG Raymond Ross from C Company who was a frequent contributor.

---0---

For all intents and purposes my arm's mobility had been restored, albeit with some pain as I mentioned in the letter to Lynne July 23rd. Hoswever issues with my shoulder and the injury linger even today in 2020. I have lived with chronic pain in my "crikky" shoulder for more than 50 years. And while my 71st Evac therapists (whom I appreciate and sincerely thank for their assistance) stated that, in their estimation, full mobility had been restored, recent (2018-2019) examinations by doctors at the VA reveal a somewhat different evaluation. My shoulder has never been "fully restored" or perhaps it has deteriorated over the years and most likely never will be "normal."

I returned to the VA Health System in 2018 to see if they could figure out why I was experiencing loss of strength, limited mobility, chronic and sometimes severe pain. After a cursory palpation exam, and without hesitation, my normal VA physician immediately prescribed Physical Therapy. He did this on that simple "touch test" before scheduling any additional examinations! I would have to wait several months before actually having any other, more conclusive tests performed. And since the VA was "backed up," a series of x-rays (here we go again) were taken by an outside provider. More Physical Therapy was prescribed again but that did not diminish the pain; we did not seem to be making any more progress than in 1968. And, I pointed out to the VA therapist, one part of the muscle in my right shoulder simply was not moving correctly—that old "crikky" thing I mentioned in the letter to Lynne, July 1968.

Finally, when the therapist palpated it while I was performing one exercise, he finally felt the odd way it moved! At last, an MRI was scheduled in January 2019 (this time back at the VA in Nashville). It revealed there was a little more going on besides the general wear and tear of Acromioclavicular Osteoarthritis. That multi-syllable tongue-tangling condition had been diagnosed by the team of outside orthopedic surgeons who earlier had examined my x-rays. In the new MRI images, the team discovered several partial tears and fraying in both the supraspinatus tendon and the infraspinatus tendon. Of course, those very well could have been recent injuries. But of even more interest to me, they found that of the rotator cuff muscles and tendons holding my shoulder in place … it appeared to them that not all were even fully attached. They could not see where -- or even if -- the long head tendon was actually attached!

In the end, they advised that I might want to consider having surgery to reattach the long head of the biceps tendon. But barring that, they also suggested the other ones "should be enough to maintain your current stability."

I really have no interest in surgery. At my age I simply do not relish the idea of going under the knife. Frankly, it makes me apprehensive. So, once again taking matters into my own hands, unless it becomes unbearably painful or significantly more immobile, I think I might just persevere with this "painful inconvenience" and constant reminder of how vulnerable our bodies can be. (Hoping that Lynne will continue to be an angel and tolerate my perpetual moans and groans.)

In the meantime, I'll continue to rely on the tried and true iART (Ice, Arnica, Rest & Tylenol).

Chapter Fourteen

"Mr. Tambourine Man"
The Byrds
(Written by Bob Dylan - 1965)

A Hodgepodge of Happenings

August 7, 1968

Virtually every single letter or note I wrote to Lynne in August 1968 had comments and enthusiastic speculation regarding taking R&R together. GIs in Vietnam were supposed to receive one week of R&R or "Rest & Recuperation" (sometimes called Rest and Relaxation or Rest and Recreation) during their 12 months' service. GIs had the option of requesting five days in Bangkok, Hong Kong, Kuala Lampur, Penang, Manila, Seoul, Singapore, Taipei and Tokyo or seven days (due to longer travel time) in Australia or Hawaii.

R&R could be requested any time after serving six months in country. Lynne and I hoped to schedule our rendezvous for September so we would have only a few months left after R&R until my ultimate return home. We hoped to meet in Hawaii but seemed to be caught in a seemingly perpetual limbo about the exact dates when our trip might actually happen. That state of uncertainty made things extremely tense and difficult for Lynne since she did not know when to make her plane reservations.

Part of the problem in pinning down a date was that someone at 1st Signal Brigade forgot to send down the monthly allotment of R&R availability dates and places for September. Thus, everybody in the organization was in a state of confused consternation.

I shared some of my frustrations and the disheartening working conditions I was struggling with in this note to Lynne.

"Tis the 7th of August, 8:05 pm and I am just finishing work. The paper is not yet to bed, there is so, so much work to do and so, so very much harassment. Would you believe I typed a "True Copy" (a copy of a letter in the most minute detail) 19 times today—Damn, was I mad....They just kept on returning it, and returning it, and returning it—for the most absurd reasons. It was supposed to be letter perfect — no smudges, no smears, no erasures, etc. Yet by the time it went through all the various channels and got to the Colonel, it was

dirty, wrinkled, smeared, smudged, and etc....as they say in Vietnamese...Dinque Dau—"Dinky Dow"—messed up, screwed up, et al."

"By the way, this letter was just interrupted for a period of one hour and fifteen minutes. Right after I typed the words, "most minute detail", the siren sounded and we went on Practice Red Alert. Boy, oh boy, is this place messed up.... People in the wrong spot, no ammo at some places, everyone trying to be the big CHIEF and everyone (except the "old timers") just running in circles. Denny Mahlstedt, Dave Morales, Bill Dailey, Joe Caserta, and Bob Kerr and I were the only ones who knew what was happening. Of course, if anything ever does happen—we won't be the ones to get the Bronze Star. Two guys killed in Kontum during the Tet Offensive, defending their compound, 26 wounded, three more killed in convoy, three more wounded in March...some haven't even gotten their purple hearts... However, everyone of the officers who DEROSED or transferred received a Bronze Star for "meritorious service against a hostile force" etc, etc—BULL. Damn, it makes me so mad I could scream. I guess the old saying, "RHIP—Rank Has Its Privileges is really true—what if they were to write the true story behind those awards??!! Can you imagine"....[In my letter to Lynne, I list specific officers from HHD whose names I will not repeat here.]...."AWARDED NATIONS'S SIXTH HIGHEST AWARD **BRONZE STAR** FOR SITTING BEHIND DESK AND PASSING THE BUCK."

"Oh to be short!"

August 13, 1968

"Got a new roommate, Jim Griffis from Beltsville, MD. He's a clean cut, really nice guy."

"Flying to Nha Trang tomorrow with Larry Fritz from S2 (Intelligence)."

One more mystery trip for me. Where I was going was noted in the letter but nothing to indicate why I was going to accompany someone from Intelligence. At least some of these trips (apparently) helped me maintain a modicum of sanity.

August 22, 1968

"Sent you the R&R orders which will allow you to travel at a lower expense."

August 23, 1968

"Sent you three sets of the R&R orders just in case any get lost in the mail.

"Dear Mrs. Kaltreider, You have won our "Birthday Girl" contest ..... a trip to Hawaii ..... commencing on September 13, 1968."

We finally had a firm date for our trip, now with only three weeks' notice.

August 27, 1968

"Tengo miedo que esta nota va estar muy, muy corto, pero se que tu sabes porque y entiendes, no? Poco a poco la poblacion de esta carcel se esta yendo a loco, mejor dicho, se está enloquiciendo. Ciento nueve mas — o menos con suerte."

"Translation: I'm afraid that this note will be very, very short, but I know that you know why and you understand, right? Little by little the population of this prison is going crazy, or rather, it is becoming crazy. One hundred and nine more — or less with luck. Tried to call yesterday - had guard (CoR) again but didn't get through."

Alas! Another failed call at headquarters of our communications unit. After this, I simply quit trying.

August 28, 1968

By now, I was given permission to write my own column in *The Unicorn* each month. That certainly helped fill some space since getting out into the field to cover stories was becoming more difficult. My column was titled "kal's korner" and it focused on a variety of things from taking your malaria pill (with plenty of sarcasm woven in) ... to a full-page editorial about *The Star Spangled Banner* with all the verses to it along with illustrations (and absolutely no sarcasm!) ... to a tongue-in-cheek history and parody of the 278th Pigeon Company that was based on a real life 1943 Signal Unit—the *1308th Signal Pigeon Company* formed in Florida as part of the 43rd Signal Battalion that served in Europe during the Second World War. I seemed to be finding a "groove" in at least one way to furtively vent some of my frustration.

Ah, but things were not, as was the vernacular back then, "copacetic." For example, the following problematic and rather contemptuous (and, upon reflection, misguided) incident almost derailed all my plans.

I sent Lynne a copy of an ill-conceived piece, an editorial of sorts that I had written for my personal column. I wanted to publish it in the next issue of *The Unicorn* so I submitted it to my editor, 1st Lt Bill Morgan. Morgan summarily rejected it (and upon reflection now -- absolutely, rightly so.) The upshot of my insistent complaining about the situation I described in the piece -- even though it was not published -- was that I was threatened with an Article 15. (An Article 15 is a punishment short of Court Martial carried out without judicial proceedings but an indelible "blot" on one's record.)

My proposed editorial listed what I considered all the "BS" flower planting and "beautification" that was going on. The list included planting grass and beds of flowers at the entrance to HQ. The colonel insisted on having the hallway that gave access to HQ offices (in our wing but not that led to S2) ... the one that ultimately led to his office -- painted. Not once. Not twice. But, three times in one week – because he did not like the "tint" of gray-green paint. Plus, he had a flower bed planted next to the private entrance to his office (the one he nearly always used).

All this was transpiring while our perimeter sat relatively "exposed" with one single strand of barbed wire strung along its length. That area also was peppered with "spider holes" dug by the Viet Cong outside the wire but which tunneled underneath to a point just inside our perimeter. (I've included a photo in the Appendix). In addition, the area adjacent to the perimeter wire included a few scattered "punji stake" pits.

Punji stake pits or traps were camouflaged depressions created to conceal dozens of upright, sharp-pointed bamboo or metal stakes. These short skewers were similar to the sharp end of a broken-off spear stuck "business end up" into the ground at the bottom of the pit or sometimes hidden in an overgrown area that was likely to be traversed by troops patrolling nearby. As for the pits outside our compound, they were very well camouflaged. The bottom of these shallow (two or three-foot depressions) held hundreds of these pointed lances waiting for an unsuspecting individual to step on them or fall into. They weren't meant to kill, but rather to maim or wound. They were especially effective in the latter since the tips were usually coated with poison from plants, animals, or more often than not, with human feces.

I have no idea how old these were, nor who installed them. They could have been left over from the French occupation since several archaic, yet formidable concrete French bunkers also remained intact along our perimeter. Considering the punji pits were outside our wire, they probably would be relatively ineffective against VC who likely mapped where they were. But they certainly posed a danger to our troops, most of whom were unaware of their existence, since virtually no one ventured along or outside the wire (save for me and a few colleagues in S2.)

All-in-all, I felt our situation in regard to our unit and its defenses, especially along the north perimeter, was an example of the Army at its worst: a lot of spit-shine and polish, old traditions and bugle calls (!) but nobody having a clue about what the hell was going on. Still, I was powerless to do anything about it. So, is it any wonder why I was becoming angry and more cynical with each passing day?

I began to slip even more cynicism into my writing and was rather sacrilegious in a portion of one paragraph I wrote for an issue of *The Unicorn*. The article, appearing on page one, was titled, "Hi-Rise at Chapel." It described how the 299th Engineer Battalion constructed a steeple for our newly constructed Chapel of Communications. The steeple was installed by several members of HHD, along with carpet that was installed by members of Company A. I specifically phrased one sentence in the published article thusly: "…. the altar carpet was laid prior to the steeple's erection…." A definite play on words with sexual innuendos fully intended.

Yes, I had become very hypocritical and insincere, teetering on the edge of sacrilege, and boldly derisive in some of my writing. However, I never – never – never wrote any unfavorable or derogatory stories about the men in our units. Above all, they were friends, colleagues, and staunch defenders of our presence in Southeast Asia. And as I saw firsthand, they were heroes in many instances. It was the proverbial Army "brass" that incurred my ire and disdain (and that of many of my friends').

Disagreements with "higher authority" has been an age-old condition in every conflict every fought, one that eventually became an ugly source of dissension in other units as the war progressed. There were instances of fragging of officers (tossing hand grenades) into their quarters and eventually, the absolute refusal of some troops to fight. The most widely reported instance of the latter occurred in August 1969 when men in Company A of the Third Battalion, 196th Light Infantry Brigade refused to continue a search mission in Que Son Valley South of Danang.

In August 1968, another significant event mirrored racial tensions that were very evident in the states. In this case, an uprising of black GIs took place at the notoriously harsh Long Binh Jail (nicknamed Camp LBJ), just outside of Saigon. Some of the soldiers who were incarcerated at LBJ had been convicted of extremely serious crimes like murder. Some were jailed for something as simple as refusing to get a haircut. Still others were there after being convicted of smoking pot, using more addictive drugs or for various and sundry crimes.

Racial tensions in the jail grew increasingly worse. Guards were infamous for treating black and white inmates very differently with the harshest punishments given to soldiers of color. And when word of Dr. Martin Luther King's assassination was received, the proverbial pot began to boil. Ultimately, it boiled over and at midnight on **August 29, 1968**, a group of prisoners charged and attacked the guards, then began dismantling the stockade. Some inmates began fighting among themselves and utter chaos ensued. A day later the military reported that everything was back under control. But that was far from the truth. A group of 12 black soldiers still controlled a section of the stockade.

They held it for nearly a week. The Army deliberately tried to keep this event from escalating any further. They even threw cases of C-Rations over the fence for the rebelling prisoners to eat.

Finally, on September 7, 1968, the Army sent in a Company of MPs from 720th Military Police Battalion. The MPs came through in a riot-formation wedge, firing teargas cannisters ahead of them. In the end, the Army continued to downplay the story as well as the mistreatment of black prisoners. But little by little, bit by bit, the truth finally came out.

As the war continued to spin out of control, the negative sentiment and dissidence so evident in the states, continued to spread among US troops in a variety of ways. Even Captain Leroy Denniston of the 459th Signal Battalion wrote a lighthearted column for *The Unicorn* that was peppered with sarcasm. I featured it on the front page of the September 1968 edition. His article, "25 Hour Day Planned," provided details about adding a 25th hour to every day because there were never enough hours in a normal day. Thus, the Army was going to fix that in its own inimitable way. It was an amusing piece that reflected the attitude many people had — a "We Gotta Get Outta This Place" frame of mind.

August 29, 1968
Lynne's Birthday!

"What a special day today!
"What a sunshine brite — a patter of rain too."
"Whither thou goest America?" [reference both to the political turmoil in the US and events in-country]

….and lots of birthday wishes scribbled and printed creatively all over the paper since I wrote and mailed it on her actual birthday.

Chapter Fifteen

"Dedicated to the One I Love"
Shirelles; Mamas & Papas
(Written by Lowman Pauling & Ralph Bass - 1959)

September 1, 1968

"Still haven't been able to get my tape recorder working." [It had been broken for more than a month.] *...and ... "They messed up our pay again - forgot to increase our allotment* [to coincide with my promotion to E5]*."*

September 6, 1968

"Today is a very happy day"....

Our plans for R&R were finally set. Lynne was going to head to Hawaii a week early and stay with Jan Walker, wife of her cousin Frank who was stationed at Pearl Harbor. Jan would introduce Lynne to the area while Frank was deployed at sea during her visit.

I, on the other hand, would be taking a 13-hour flight scheduled to arrive in Honolulu on the 13th. I sent Lynne a sheet of instructions about the R&R Center that was published by the military and distributed to all personnel going on R&R in Hawaii. These instructions included specific guidelines and an admonition about not coming to the airport to meet the plane. It designated a specific area to stand and wait at the R&R Center...details, details, details.

By this time in my tour (mid-September) I had helped write and publish 7 monthly newspapers, done perhaps a dozen radio interviews, researched, written, and forwarded more than 213 news releases for distribution. I had noted these numbers in a letter to my parents. And, in return, my mother who was a secretary at Keystone-AAA Insurance Company in York, expressed her surprise in a letter to me, "Oh, my goodness, that must have taken a lot of typing!" Yes, Mom, it did.

So now, considering my frenetic, hop-scotch schedule across and up and down the highlands of South Vietnam, I was more than ready for R&R! But more importantly, I was simply, unequivocally desperate to see Lynne.

September 13, 1968

Friday the 13th became a symbol of *Good Luck* rather than bad luck for Lynne and me when we enthusiastically and blissfully met in Honolulu for R&R on this date. After enduring a 10-month separation it became an incredibly memorable day we will cherish forever because of the multitude of happy, playful, and intimate moments we shared and the warm, wonderful memories we hold dear from that day and the all-too-short week that followed.

We stayed at the Reef Hotel on Waikiki Beach for $14 a night! The hotel staff was welcoming, deferential, and very accommodating to GIs and their families on R&R. From what we saw, nearly all of these guests were spouses as opposed to families with children.

Strolling in the sand and basking in the warm sun of Hawaii turned out to be true heaven on earth for us. We spent every waking and sleeping moment together and did very little "tourist" stuff other than to tour the USS Arizona Memorial at Pearl Harbor. Strangely, the boat ride from the dock to the Memorial turned out to be another very brief reunion of sorts. Seated across from us was a sailor (also on R&R) who had been a high school classmate of mine, Neal Fetter. Small world!

And then all too soon, the week came to an end and Lynne and I parted.

Just over a week after that dreams-do-come-true in Paradise trip I wrote an excited, verbally animated letter.

SNAFU & FUBAR – It's the Army Way
(Translation: Situation Normal All Fucked Up & Fucked Up Beyond All Recognition, two acronyms originating in the military during WWII.)

September 24, 1968

"You're not going to believe this but— HOW WOULD YOU LIKE TO GO ON R&R AGAIN THE 22ND OF OCTOBER TO THE 29TH????????

[Yes, I printed that line in all caps in the letter to Lynne.]

"No, I'm not drunk, nor joking. A once-in-a year fluke has come up and there is an extra allocation for the 22nd of October..."

Without going into many details, a few thoughtful and sensible paragraphs later I wrote, *"Would you believe that I just talked myself out of another R&R ... unless YOU WANT TO?" .....*

In the end we chose not to take advantage of this unusual opportunity. Lynne was working full-time and going to grad school, and we were trying to save money for starting our life together after my return.

And then, believe it or not ... in the Army's inexplicable fashion, two more odd situations unfolded with respect to R&R.

First: Right before my shoulder injury, I was granted permission to remodel the Information Office and add a darkroom. I scrounged materials and bartered for supplies from 4th Infantry Division and began to build the project: wall dividers, worktables, printer and sink areas, cabinets, and the like ... by myself ... in my "spare time." I begged and borrowed and connived with friends in supply and maintenance to acquire tools. I drew plans for hooking up to the water supply, although admittedly, wastewater was an unresolved issue. I even went so far as to go on a nearly disastrous convoy to Qui Nhon to pick up some of the materials we needed.

But ... when I got back from R&R, our CO, LTC Motsko, asked my immediate superior, 1LT Bill Morgan, how the project was coming along. (Apparently the CO could not walk down the hall to check for himself. He almost always used his private, flower-adorned entrance.) Morgan responded, "Not finished yet, sir."

The CO's response? "Well, if I had known that, I wouldn't have let Kaltreider go on R&R!" As I mentioned before, this particular CO and I did not see eye to eye on any level whatsoever

Second: Stranger than fiction, I was offered a third opportunity to go on R&R — this time to Thailand. What the ...? There were guys in country who never had a chance to go anywhere during their stint in Vietnam.

I declined the offer. Besides, it's likely I would not have been allowed to go anyway. I had a multitude of friends in many places ... but certainly not at the end of the hallway.

September 30, 1968

The military antics of another *Catch-22* style day filled my next letter to Lynne.

"I'm in a sort of nasty mood tonight. Today was just horrendous. As usual, it began at 7:15...of course it didn't begin right; there was no water with which to shave. And then all I did was type and argue on the phone with Group [21st *Signal Group] on and off all day long regarding an award that was supposed to be given to a soldier in May. One problem... he was killed in May. But they couldn't understand that!!!"*

"And we got paid and I should be happy about that. However, it brought about my second headache—I got paid too much....the Army lost my allotment statement—who knows when?...they paid my allotment for last month and this month....SO, HON PLEASE SEND ME LAST MONTH'S PAY VOUCHER PLUS THE STATEMENT THAT SAYS, "CLASS Q ALLOTMENT

STOPPED IN JUNE. 325 CLASS L BEGIN AUGUST….. or words to that effect…..in the meantime I've put the (extra) money in the [company] safe and will keep it there….Have you been getting your checks?…."

October 15, 1968 (This is the date I wrote at the top of this letter.)

*"WOW! I goofed on that. Today's date is actually **October 4th**. I guess I was daydreaming. Got your letter #165 today. Work here is horrid. We still haven't gotten a typist so since Joe is tied up with a multitude of Article 15s, the burden falls on me and I am snowed under. Still waiting to hear your reaction to another R&R. We still could go, but you'll agree w/me and say ' 'wow', neat idea but we <u>do</u> have patience and we'll make it."*

"Tis fall, indeed. Today I saw a flock of birds. The first time I've seen any since arriving. They were going <u>West</u>."

---0---

October 14, 1968

"Last evening we heard on the news that one of the astronauts caught a cold and before I knew it I blurted out, 'They'll probably all come down with it.' And I didn't even intend to pun there. I guess some days are all just Mondays."

October 16, 1968

By now I had received specific information regarding where my new assignment would be in the states when I returned from Vietnam. But I had not yet said where we were headed in my letters to Lynne. This really irritated Lynne's father who sent me a letter that included this line.

> *"You are driving Lynne crazy. Please write and tell her where you are going to be stationed!"*

My clues were difficult and sometimes obtuse, so I decided it was time to reveal where we would be stationed when I got home.

"Decided to give you a substantially large portion of the "clues" tonight."

"California Frequently Ordered In October Often Tastes Like Ripe Alfalfa and…..the name of the unit (but no cheating by asking where it is or looking it up) … The United States Army Combat Development Command Experimentation Center."

"No, it's not as ominous as it sounds. I'm going there as an Information Specialist, perhaps to write releases on new equipment."

"Really Never Reaches Age in December and that's the total clue."

"So take the first letter of all the words, rearrange them - you get the unit (already given)."

"We are going to ... "<u>Fort Ord</u>, <u>California</u>."

"Assume it will take us 5 - 7 days. I think you should go to AAA and get them to map out the easiest route (or most expeditious). We'll have to think of accommodations along the way (tho that's not too serious.)"

There was no GPS to guide us in 1968. Instead, we planned to rely on AAA "Triptiks." Those individually-custom-made booklets consisted of spiral-bound steno notebook-size pages, each showing portions of roadway highlighted for our trip. Detours were marked as well and added to the individually segmented portions of the triptik at the last minute by local AAA office staff. They used ball-point pens to add notes or suggestions, light blue markers to indicate the recommended routes, and yellow highlighters to show road closures or construction projects. These were updated as late as possible - right before handing you the information packet. Beyond large multi-fold maps which they also included, it was the best way to get routes, detours, and turn-by-turn guidance back then. And with no "hotels.com" or "Travelocity," internet or cell phones, etc., we used AAA Travel Guides (books that were included with the maps package). These books included lists of hotels and reviews describing their "diamond rating" plus roadside and city attractions for each state. We planned to use pay phones at restaurants or in our motel along the way to call ahead for reservations on our cross-country journey.

---0---

October 21, 1968

"Dearest Love, Most Cherished Wife — More Beloved Than Any Other.

*And into the warm nite let us steal to pause the moment dreamed of quite often, before when it was only a dream.
And smile back upon one summer's morning — a breeze touched on
the face of love so held — as close as the throbbing of one's breast —*

*Assuredly that truth we know, Rightfully that trust and care. And too, not to be unmindful of the morrow lest it come upon us like the drench of
Springtime's shower.
Yet, even that is cleansing Ah! But how we know that!*

*Come, dawn; come early lite to chase away the eve's starlite. Come, dawn to burst
upon the dew of morn's sleepy-eyed mists and
break upon the eyes and ears as the rush of tide highly flung.*

*Come, dawn come, bright.
And we shall greet thee, the 'morrow — wiser, respectfully — Desired if it be some caution to the wind — but most of*

*All — come to Spring and Summer and Autumn and Wintertide to laugh on
the face of children.*

*Come. children — together we shall laugh and romp.
Together we shall — come the dawn — rush to the edges of the Earth*

*Cheer in our eyes,
Laughter in our songs, Concern on our minds
Love in our hearts.*

*Come, dawn, come love.
To the East then — together.*

October 21, 1968

Lynne also has a gift with words and it's fascinating to read a letter she wrote to me on that very same day:

> *"Dearest, From a letter from you of one year ago: --*
>
> *A mellow-gold glow, spread thru the field dotted by the crackling cornstalk mounds and dotted too by the pumpkin now ripe.*
> *A crisp tingling to the air—someone has harvested this year's crop of leaves and has now ignited their nest. The smoke billows upward and away. Distant listeners shall soon share their beauty --if only the odor of their fire – soon gone, too soon.*
> *Next year'll be another harvest – another season for the orange of the moon to match the radiance of the jack-o-lantern, another chance to romp and fall in mounds of leaves or stir pheasants from their brood in the cornfields.*
> *Walk with me. Hold my hand and we'll stroll the meadows to autumn – as one ..... always."*

Lynne added the following to my words she quoted above:

> *"And this Autumn 1968 is now at hand.*
> *The leaves have begun to turn, and yet this year*
> *They are not so gold nor orange, but are*
> *quickly turning brown to herald the approach*
> *of winter.*
> *Next autumn we shall share, but for now*
> *I wish for winter and the return of my beloved.*
> *All, Lynne*
>
> *PS 53 days, LL"*

October 24, 1968

"Love, you know now where we're going — the new question is when? Well, somehow or another we got "chumped" and have only 31-1/2 days of leave left.....I'll request "no drop" [a trade off against my time in Vietnam taken from leave I had earned] *.....I'll probably arrive in the states the 13th or 14th. Then we'll take 25 days of leave, plus 1 or 2 days travel time .... leaving the 2nd of January and then have just about a full week to drive to California."*

October 27, 1968

"47 to go. Am sort of blue tonite. Got my replacement....at least ... a temporary one. Seems he was in the Army, got a Hardship Discharge and then was Redrafted! Damn Army! He's a real nice guy - home is Ogden, Utah, name Coral Meir."

I tried to maintain my personal routine of writing to Lynne every chance I got, almost always several times a week. But for a few days, I simply was unable to do so.

November 1, 1968

"Dearest— I believe that by the time you get this you will have already sent me a "nastygram" or the like asking why I haven't written or what's wrong. Love, please forgive me but I really couldn't write until tonite and tell thee all."

"On Tuesday morning (the 29th) Tom Kane, Joe Califano (both from personnel), five other individuals and I were spirited to the VIP pad of the Pleiku airport from where we embarked on a journey to An Khe, After arriving in An Khe on our own "private" plane (!) we settled down to process in a new unit. Since this operation was classified until yesterday, I had no way of telling thee where I was or what I was doing. And even if I had ... I feared you might worry since An Khe was attacked by considerable force the same night we got there. In fact, one storage dump was still burning when we left. Anyhow, I went and have returned safe and sound. You can read about it in the next Unicorn...if it gets published." [It did.]

We actually processed the arrival of men in two new units to Vietnam—the 270th Signal Company and the 17th Signal Platoon. We did this to avoid the perpetual log jam at Cam Ranh Bay and Bien Hoa (near Saigon) and our work got these guys into the field quickly.

"I used my last roll of outdated film and not one single picture turned out!"

November 13-15

I wrote only 8 more times from Vietnam. In those letters and notes I told Lynne a few more details about my last (now, unclassified) mission to An Khe, a few details about our upcoming assignment at Fort Ord. I also told her I sold my sound equipment for $300.

I repeated myself innumerable times in the hastily scribbled letters without adding anything of substance. I gave instructions about preparing for the transport of our household goods (mostly hers) to California by the Army; and asked her not to write any letters after the 6th or 8th of December. I mentioned gifts of Montagnard crossbows for some of our family members. When I did return to the states, I brought only one of those home for us and a rather fascinating but strange wooden Montagnard người bắt, a small animal catcher (a very unusual kind of mousetrap).

November 18, 1968

"Well, here's change 394 to change 78 to change 366" [Simply my nonsense regarding the Army's constantly changing of my orders to return home.]"

"Do not write after November 30th!"

"Still trying to coordinate with John. As soon as I get into Fort Lewis, I'll call you and tell you all the details."

November 20, 1968

"John phoned last night and said that he's got his flight - H2C4 leaving Cam Ranh Bay for the USA at 1320 hours (1:20 pm) on the 7th of December!"

"I will close for tonight with "Happy Anniversary."

My hastily scribbled notes did little to alleviate Lynne's growing concern as we grew "shorter." ("Short Timer" was the nickname given to someone who had less than a month left to serve. We even had "Short Timer" calendars to mark off the remaining days. These were similar to Advent Calendars, most of which -- at least in-country -- were filled with bawdy images.)

Meanwhile, Lynne's notes to me hinted that our pending assignment in California was becoming more appealing to her. Yet, those notes also revealed a growing uneasiness regarding my personal safety. News reports in the states continued to cover increased enemy attacks in the Pleiku area. Several of her notes expressed how frightened she felt by these attacks. Her apprehension, after a pressure-filled nearly 12 months apart, was compounded by not knowing where in Pleiku these attacks were taking place, or if I might be near any of them. Her concerns were well-founded, especially in light of my frequent travel in-country and the letter at the beginning of November describing my trip to An Khe. Lynne literally pleaded with me to try and find some way to get home sooner, even trading leave time and missing Christmas if that were possible. (It wasn't.)

Wednesday, November 20th

> *Pleiku hit again! Please, please hurry, hurry home. I love you. I LOVE YOU. All...ever! Lynne.*
> *PS 23 days tomorrow.*

November 23, 1968

"Would you believe that we've now got just <u>two weeks</u> left?"

"Port calls came down today and altho I couldn't get on the same flight as John, I got the same day. The word:

My flight info:

Seaboard World Airlines
Flight G2C4
Leaving CRB 11:30 am
7 Dec 68

---0---

November 26, 1968

"Spoke to John today and after pulling some strings, I got him booked on the same flight as me."

November marked the start of the 2nd year of publication of *The Unicorn*. It was my last issue.

It also contained my final sarcastic "filler" in the form of a tongue-in-cheek block advertisement.

"PANAVISION PARK"
Now Open to the Public Daily 0700 to 1800
(Enemy Permitting)

SEE: Charming Pleiku City
The Verdant Oasis
The Awesome Cambodian Border
The Scenic 4th Infantry Division Base Camp Dump

ADMISSION————————FREE
(Bring your weapon)

Located on panoramic Dragon Mountain in Pleiku
Branches in An Khe and Dak To

I'm pleased to say that my friends from the 278th Signal Company who ran our station on Dragon Mountain (actually overlooking 4th Infantry Division's Camp Enari and the valley South of the city) appreciated the silly 'tip of the hat.' They understood … and … they "got it."

Chapter Sixteen

"If I Had a Hammer"
Peter, Paul, & Mary; Trini Lopez
(Written by Pete Seeger & Lee Hays - 1949)

Civic Action Program
Our unit's contributions "Beyond War"

During the months following Tet, whenever our Commanding Officer, Col Leo DuBeau went on local goodwill inspections...aka photo-ops, I was right there alongside him, snapping photographs and taking notes for follow-up articles. A few times these events also were attended by our Executive Officer, Major Edward Raleigh, our Chaplain, Captain Thomas Denson, plus our Battalion Sergeant Major. Sergeant Major Edward Rogers often "choreographed" these trips (in a good way), making sure we had smiling locals and ARVN soldiers placed prominently in the photos or in the background. He even arranged to have bouquets of flowers to be handed to some of the local women whose homes were being rebuilt. The excursions were to places where we had completed construction projects or were in the process of rebuilding homes that had been damaged or completely destroyed during the Tet Offensive. In reality, all of our units across the Central Highlands participated in Civic Action activities, some unit sponsored, some initiated by individuals within the units.

Similar to C Company's work with the Montagnards in Kontum that I mentioned in a previous chapter, some of our men became pseudo surrogate "fathers" for the Holy Infant Orphanage in An Khe. Some examples of their involvement and care include our guys digging a well for fresh water for them, repairing the roof of the orphanage, and donating charcoal for cooking. A spouse of one of the men of the 586th Signal Company collected and shipped clothing, personal hygiene supplies, and blankets as gifts for the orphanage in An Khe.

Meanwhile in Pleiku, SP5 Mike Pauli from A Company worked with his wife to organize a clothing drive for Montagnard children in the villages not far from our compound. Likewise, monetary donations were collected for the Pleiku Leprosarium near Camp Enari, south of the city. And men from the 43rd donated food for at least one other of the four Montagnard villages in our area.

Our men donated money for construction materials and helped build homes for teachers plus made repairs at a school in Pleiku for dependents of our counterpart Vietnamese Signal Unit in II Corps. (II Corps was the designation for our Operational Area in the Central Highlands.) These trips and activities were set up to help show that our mission in Vietnam was more than just communications. Some of the articles I wrote following these trips were published in *The Unicorn* while many articles and accompanying photos were forwarded to 1st Signal Brigade and US Army Information for their records and for wider distribution.

Without a doubt, of all the things I did in Vietnam, I enjoyed these assignments the most. The projects were something for which I had a great personal affinity. I enjoyed visiting the school we built both during construction and at the dedication. The latter was a very festive event with US and South Vietnamese military attending and dozens of beautiful smiling children. At first, the children played games while waiting for the ceremonies to begin. Then they performed a song or two and a dance for us. Last, they gave us small tokens of appreciation in the form of handmade art and craft decorations they had created.

In many ways, these assignments, specifically, the Civic Action program, were "near and dear" to my heart, projects to which I could truly relate. I especially liked visiting the Jarai and Rhade (tribes) Montagnard Villages. All of these visits affected me almost as if they were a vicarious continuation of my work as a Peace Corps Volunteer in Colombia. I felt a distinct kinship to these hard-working, simple people. Their bamboo homes were built on platforms several feet above the ground, except in some of the resettlement camps. In many ways these trips reminded me of the year I spent living in a house with thatched roof in Nilo, Cundinamarca, my first year in South America. The one significant difference was that my bamboo and wattle and daub hut was built right on the ground and subject to anything that creeped or slithered or crawled. In another Montagnard village I saw examples of communal longhouses with high peaked thatched roofs also built on stilt platforms, similar to some of the homes built along waterways in the Amazon. I was strangely comfortable here …. even in the middle of the war zone. But, in a sense, that feeling of affability was woefully misplaced.

The Montagnard's differing culture and distinctive dress set them apart from the "ordinary" Vietnamese. According to some researchers, at one time 30 indigenous tribes with separate language and customs lived in Vietnam and neighboring Laos. These people were mistreated and discriminated against repeatedly, first by the French and later by the Vietnamese. They were often derogatively labeled "Moi" or "savage" by the Vietnamese. Teaching or promoting or even encouraging the use of their native language was forbidden during much of Vietnam's history. The Montagnards were treated with an inordinate amount of disrespect and much disdain, just like Native Americans tribes were treated by white settlers in the United States. Yet the Montagnards were staunch defenders of their tribal lands and fought against the Viet Cong and North Vietnamese Regulars at a very high cost in lives lost, all-the-while allied with the US. The affinity I felt for the Vietnamese, most especially toward the Montagnards, was evident in some measure in my personal efforts to secure assistance for them outside official military channels. But just as it was for me in South America, my efforts fell far short of fulfillment.

---0---

As I reflect upon my time in Vietnam -- the countless trips, the myriad interviews, the fun photo assignments, even though many times they were completed under duress -- I sadly encounter many total blanks. Few physical mementoes remain to refresh my memory, and only a few letters and official documents related to my duties survived like the one quoted earlier from Al Dawson. Unfortunately, no actual interview notes exist from any of my trips. The latter were either left behind or accidently destroyed, along with many of my paper records and photos from South America when they were inadvertently stored in my old footlocker in our barn in PA. I don't know if any of my "Hometown Hero" audio recordings exist. I even contacted American Forces Vietnam Network (AFVN) in 2020 and was informed that they never made any attempt to archive any of these specific recordings, especially since they had been done on vinyl tape and were much too hard to preserve. Regrettably gone but not forgotten by all.

Some details of my work are missing from my fading memory due to the normal aging process, some passing through my memory as unintelligible wisps of amorphous clouds. Others I simply cannot summon -- or subconsciously choose not to awaken from their sleep. I cannot recall any specific purpose for my visits to these villages or to some of the remote sites, other than for the community action work, very little of which was done with the Montagnards. It truly is a perplexing mystery to me.

When I repeatedly read and reread the ten monthly unit newspapers that I published during my year in Pleiku, some articles came back vividly, evoking visual memories along with some deep-seated feelings, a few with lucid specifics of the incidents or excursions. Yet, others stubbornly remained lost in a complete fog. Whether I have blocked these out - as I have often believed – or simply forgotten, I simply cannot answer. Certainly, I choose not to share some of the more graphic things I can recall about my time in Vietnam.

I'm certain that if I had any photos or notes, even just a few from some of these trips, they would help immensely. Unfortunately, many could well have been classified after I took them and retained by the Army. I also believe some of what I considered my personal shots were kept by someone in our unit, a person who I used as a photo courier at times.

One very specific instance stands out as oddly suspicious. It happened with the last batch of three rolls taken over a period of several days in the Montagnard villages. They were supposed to be returned to me, but the person delivering them was (apparently) suddenly sent on TDY. I know he admired and frequently spoke highly of my photos. Unfortunately, I never saw any of them—nor him again. But then, it's possible they could have ended up anywhere. This was a convoluted and confusing time in many, many ways.

I was under the impression that our (my) presence in these villages was to document the assistance we were providing to the Montagnards. Indeed, we accomplished quite a bit of that in Pleiku, Kontum, and Ban Me Thuot. But there very well could have been other things afoot that I was not privy to since the 43rd also provided support for MACV (Military Assistance Command Vietnam), some highly classified ops, specifically communications support for the SOG (Special Operations Group, later known as Studies and Observations Group). These special forces units secretly monitored traffic on the Ho Chi Minh Trail and also were part of rescue, a prisoner snatch, plus other activities associated with US secret warfare across the border with Laos and Cambodia and all along the trail that led literally to our back door. And in those small, very remote camps I visited like the Special Forces Camp at Plei Djereng and Tram, west of Pleiku - near the Cambodian border, we did not conduct any Civic Action projects. I simply am at a loss to fill in the voids.

Chapter Seventeen

"Ticket To Ride"
The Beatles
(Written by John Lennon & Paul McCartney 1965)

Odds and Ends
And a Bit of Not-So-Official Army Life

A handful of times a senior NCO asked me to drive him (off the record) into the city of Pleiku. There, he had rented an unofficial "residence" and supported a "personal" Mama San (sometimes derogatorily nicknamed a "moose") whom he enjoyed visiting. Uh, ... note, she wasn't doing his laundry. This was unequivocally against Army Regulations, but it was something that was kept close to the vest and never discussed publicly. A whole lot of "what the army doesn't know won't hurt them" seemed to be going on just about everywhere. And it seems to have happened in virtually every conflict in which the US and most likely other countries have been involved.

I'd drop the Master Sergeant off, then sit outside in the jeep waiting with rifle in hand. This served two purposes: one, simply to insure no one stole the jeep while he was meeting with his Vietnamese mistress and, two, to always be on the lookout and prepared for "whatever" in case we had to hightail it back to the compound. Fortunately, that "whatever" never seemed to come during his "business" visits. And, invariably, an extra drink was waiting at the bar for me when we returned to the compound, courtesy of this benefactor who shall remain anonymous.

One other sadly damning note about this individual; he was an alcoholic. And he nearly was shot by friendly fire as he staggered toward the perimeter defense line one night while we were under attack. He kept shouting "Don't shoot, it's me. Don't shoot!" while stumbling, weaving, and bumbling his way toward us. When he finally fell through the bunker door onto his face, we decided to just let him lie there. What was happening outside the wire was of more importance than a passed-out drunk.

My trips by jeep at other times around Pleiku were taken to beg, barter, or scrounge any materials we were short of and needed in a hurry. During these trips, I was able to sit in the passenger's seat, albeit armed and always on the lookout, with a driver to escort me. Most of that kind of trip was to the 4th Infantry Division HQ at Camp Enari, south of the city. Those guys invariably seemed to be willing to share just about anything and they were always willing to lend a hand any way they could. So, to them, a belated salute: Go Big Ivy; "Steadfast and Loyal."

A few trips I took were to areas slightly north of our compound near Lake Bien Hoa. I scoured all of these areas for any GI-associated human-interest stories or local events that might possibly be a part of the "Hearts and Minds" pacification program that President Johnson was trying to push. A big problem with that program was that, while the purpose was to convince the Vietnamese to support their own South Vietnamese government, our military operations of "search and destroy" had the opposite effect. South Vietnamese villages invariably were infiltrated by Viet Cong who had their own despicable and dastardly methods of persuasion as well. While the Vietnamese who worked in our compounds appeared relatively friendly during the day, many turned unfriendly at night. Sometimes it was the only way to survive this confusing conflict. They were threatened and cajoled and intimidated by both sides - US and NVA/Viet Cong alike. And horribly, sometimes they or their families were tortured or simply assassinated by the enemy, instilling fear and eliminating any hardcore "sympathizers" of President Nguyễn Văn Thiệu.

From December 1967 through December 1968 while I was in Pleiku, we never had a ground assault on our compound. However, our classified intelligence reports indicated an assault of Viet Cong and NVA was being planned for both late January 1968 and May 1968. And while we were harassed occasionally by rocket and mortar fire, especially during Tet, the 4th Infantry Division kept us well defended. The 4th was one of the many units for which we were helping provide communications support. Tanks from the 69th Armor Regiment were stationed nearby while 4th Division ground troops were on alert not far from Tropo Hill and the 43rd Compound. First Battalion, 92nd Artillery was positioned slightly north of us. Their guns were often aimed to fire on Viet Cong and NVA positions in the mountains also just a few miles north.

In contrast to our status in Pleiku, 43rd Signal Battalion units in Kontum, Dak To, Ban Me Thuot, An Khe, and even Nha Trang as well as a few other communication sites were susceptible to ground assault or attack by sappers who usually were armed with explosives. These stealthy commandos used a variety of means to breach our perimeter defenses. Those remote camps also were subjected to harassing mortar and rocket attacks almost any time of the day and night.

Periodically we would hear rumors that the Viet Cong were using our large (120 foot and 60 foot tall) Tropo screens - located on the small hill behind our barracks in Pleiku - to help aim their fire. Perhaps that's one reason the screens themselves never seemed to be targeted even though enemy shells landed in the compounds on every side around them. Pleiku airfield was hit frequently. And in February 1968, the 71st Evac hospital right next to us was shelled, killing one patient and causing additional casualties to the staff and injured soldiers already being cared for there.

Our compound near Pleiku was considered to be reasonably safe, yet it still was likely that Viet Cong had infiltrated or had spies on our base. This became abundantly clear when one of our men was stabbed in the Mess Hall kitchen by a VC (or VC sympathizer) — during daylight hours no less. As Pleiku City became increasingly more dangerous, it was declared totally "Off Limits" and unapproachable during Tet as well as for a short time thereafter. Fortunately, about a month and a half after Tet, things loosened up a bit, and we were allowed to go back into certain parts of the city. Nonetheless, it remained a dangerous place and "Off-Limits" at night.

Chapter Eighteen

"King of the Road"
Roger Miller
(Written by Roger Miller 1964)

The Rides of My Life

Most of the trips I took outside of Pleiku other than by jeep or truck were in "Hueys," the *Bell UH-1D Iroquois that* was used extensively throughout Vietnam. The ones we flew in were part of the 1st Signal Brigade's "mini air force" which consisted of 15 aircraft. Later in the war, and after I left Vietnam, this number grew to 45 aircraft. These were used to provide quick access and to resupply remote communication sites run by our unit plus other groups we assisted under the 1st Signal Brigade command structure. I absolutely loved flying in the Hueys and got to know several pilots and crew fairly well. One of our pilots even offered to let me fly along in the co-pilot's seat when he was about to return the aircraft from the chopper pad near the 43rd Compound to the more secure revetments at Camp Holloway. But my immediate superior, 1LT Morgan, steadfastly refused to let me go. I'm pretty sure he was jealous of the offer. Xin lỗi, quá tệ (So sorry, too bad.)

The Hueys we flew in were "slicks," meaning they were used primarily for troop and material transport and only had basic armament of 2, M-60 machine guns - one mounted on each side. All of us wore flak jackets, but a number of guys sat on theirs if they were staying on the chopper for any length of time. They sat on them for extra protection from ground fire since hostiles could fire up at us through the thin fuselage and undercarriage at any time we were in the air, especially flying at treetop level.

Once in a while a guy would go to the extent of sitting on his helmet, inverted to deflect any rounds. But I kept both my flak jacket and helmet on since I was literally jumping on and off the chopper and had little concern while airborne.

I had the opportunity to fly on several fixed-wing aircraft to some assignments. Two of the fixed-wing planes I hitched rides on were a C-130 transport and one C-123 that had transported Agent Orange. This was on one of my trips to Nha Trang where Operation Ranch Hand, the defoliation project, was headquartered. Other than the one trip aboard that specific aircraft, I was fortunate not to be exposed to those horrible, cancer-causing chemicals. Agent Orange (2,4,5-T and 2,4-D with Dioxin as (at least) one of the cancer-causing ingredients) was sprayed via a variety of fixed-wing aircraft, helicopters, and even by hand. It was one of the biggest errors of the war and inflicted unintentional casualties on all sides of the conflict. The awful effects linger on today - 50 years later -- in survivors and sadly, also in their children and even their grandchildren.

One other really fascinating fixed-wing aircraft that took me on assignment to An Khe was a *de Havilland Canada DHC-4 Caribou*, a STOL (Short Take Off & Landing) tactical cargo plane. In Vietnam it was used as a cargo and troop carrier that could get in and out of tight places very quickly. It took off and landed at amazing acute angles that felt like we were going nearly straight up and straight down! This allowed the plane to avoid most ground fire as it landed or took off.

I also flew in a *de Havilland Canada* DHC-2 Beaver, a small single engine plane that can carry up to seven people. The trip in that aircraft was between Pleiku and Qui Nhon via the Mang Yang Pass during a hell of a storm. It was the one time flying in Vietnam that scared me the most - pretty much to the point that I wasn't sure we were going to make it through safely.

The crosswinds we flew through had this little plane zig-zagging, pitching, and yawing at extreme angles where sometimes it felt like we were flying sideways as well as more than 60 degrees on our side. I was very happy when we landed safely! I don't even remember the info/photo assignment I was on for that trip. (Likely a follow up to the arrival of our new units in An Khe that I previously had helped process in country.) Nonetheless, I do remember there was at least one NCO – a relatively new, bombastic Sergeant Major - and a couple of officers also were on that trip. We were all belted in and hanging on for dear life. And even though I was nervous, I was forced by pride to temper my overriding bemusement at the white-knuckle, deathly pale look one newbie lieutenant had. "Scared shitless and turning green" would be a much better description of his appearance. He was petrified.

The Mang Yang Pass between Pleiku and Qui Nhon (via An Khe) was not an easy or pleasant trip by air or by ground. Route 19, only partially paved and thoroughly riddled with potholes, had gained notoriety as the place of the last official battle, indeed the turning point in the First Indochina War. In 1954 the Viet Minh wiped out the elite French *Groupement Mobile No. 100 Regimental Task Force*, destroying its equipment and every piece of the unit's artillery in this very corridor. The relative steep incline on both sides of the narrow pass forced all heavily loaded supply trucks to climb slowly in low gear, thereby creating an ideal target for snipers and other harassing attacks. The area soon became known as "Ambush Alley" due to the repeated mining of the roadway and firefights that the VC mounted here.

I traveled this extremely dangerous highway by road vehicle twice - once in each direction in a Deuce and a Half, the 2½-ton truck. This four-hour trip ended up being one of the scariest trips I took anywhere and it proved nearly disastrous.

During this particular trip, I was headed to Qui Nhon to scrounge photo chemicals and any equipment or supplies I could find so I could finish building and begin stocking my own photo lab at the 43rd. Up until that time I had to make arrangements at MACV or (usually) the Air Force darkroom at Pleiku Airbase to process any film I took. If I couldn't process it there, the film had to be sent off to Army photo services, and I never could be sure I would get the film back. Additionally, I had no guarantee -- when sent off -- that the processing unit would print the size photos I needed. And they would not know whether to crop out any portion of the prints. So, I got permission to build my own darkroom. I had learned photo processing in high school and thus, having my own darkroom would speed up things for me and provide an extra layer of security to help insure I got all the photos back and in the format needed for publication.

The cab of our truck was open, its canvas top folded back and tied down. And at one point on the 110-mile return trip, I really had to pee. So, I climbed over the back of the cab, around the gear we had scrounged from an Army surplus warehouse in Qui Nhon, and I moved to the very back of the truck. I leaned one leg against the tailgate and the other against the side rail to steady myself while the truck was flying along QL19, a road with little or no shoulder and dense, unforgiving jungle on both sides. I relieved myself....and without warning, the truck relieved itself — of me! I was thrown off when we hit a series of potholes my driver tried to avoid by swerving.

In the virtual blink of an eye I found myself in an unspeakable predicament, on my ass, tumbling on the ground, tall stands of bamboo and thick vegetation confronting me by the side of this notorious road just west of the Mang Yang Pass. I was suddenly stranded with only a 45-caliber pistol strapped to my side and a shrapnel vest on for protection. I scrambled to retrieve my helmet that had rolled along the roadway as the other trucks in the convoy continued to whiz by (no pun intended). I tried repeatedly to flag someone down to pick me up. But nobody really wanted to stop. Standing orders were not to stop under any circumstances except at MP check points. Compounding my plight was the fact that no one appeared to even want to slow down. No one wanted to become a sitting target on "the gauntlet," an isolated part of this nefarious road slightly northwest of Dak Rot Kret.

To my relief and good fortune, a guy driving an M35 2½-ton 6x6 fuel truck loaded with several thousand gallons of diesel fuel slowed just enough for me to run alongside and grab the mirror that stuck out near to the exhaust stack on the passenger side. I hauled myself up onto the running board and hung on for dear life as he sped up again.

I reached back and grabbed the vertical handhold mounted just behind the door handle with my left hand as he increased speed and continued down the road at about 40 miles an hour. I eased my way back on the running board then grabbed the door handle, opening it enough to squeeze inside whereupon the driver asked a peculiar question. "Where ya goin', buddy?"

Considerably shaken, I stared at him in disbelief, then breathlessly gasped, "Where ... ever in the fuck ... you're goin', man!"

I had time to explain to him what had happened as we drove along towards the checkpoint that the US Army's Company B, 504th Battalion "Road Runners" had set up several miles ahead. The "Road Runners" patrolled and escorted convoys on Highway 19 (East-West) between Phu Tai Valley, Qui Nhon and their base at Camp Schmidt, Pleiku, as well as on Highway 14 (North-South) from Pleiku to Kontum.

My original driver also had stopped at this checkpoint which was located near a Montagnard village (probably CP-30A several miles east of Pleiku.) I asked him, "What the hell were you doing?" (I'm curious what story he told the MPs.) He told me he didn't realize I had fallen off since he was concentrating so much on keeping pace with the convoy and trying to miss the inumerable potholes that dotted the road nearly its entire length. My immediate thought was, "Buddy it's pretty damn obvious you didn't miss many." Still trying to grasp what had just happened, he said, "I kinda wondered what was taking you so long." (I was sightseeing, asshole!)

My heart still pounds and my blood pressure rises noticeably when I pause to think of that day and what could have happened - except by the Grace of God or once again, by unexplainable, sheer dumb luck.

Chapter Nineteen

"House of the Rising Sun"
The Animals (1964)
(Traditional Folk Song)

Other Notes - Other Characters

There was a lot of personnel turnover in mid-late 1968 and one of the arrivals was a new Company First Sergeant at HHD. First Sergeant Jackson was uncommonly congenial, always encouraging, and very supportive of everyone. A jovial Southerner by birth, he always appeared to use the most amusing expressions, *"Goll durn it,"* and *"Bob Wire"* instead of "Barbed Wire." And he invariably greeted everyone, all the time as cheerfully as if they were an old friend. With his deep southern drawl, he'd ask, *"How y'all been?"* as if he hadn't seen us in a while. I was always pleasantly amused by that and by his surprising, consistently upbeat affability, especially coming from a "Regular Army Lifer," a real down-to-earth career soldier.

David Sinclair -- Company Clerk who was bitten by a rat while asleep in his bunk in our hootch and had to undergo a series of painful antirabies shots. We all took extra care to tuck in our mosquito nets draped over our bunks after that incident.

Dave Clemens -- Colonel's driver and a friend who escorted me around Pleiku several times.

Sergeant Bill Dailey -- great guy and friend. He's the person who called out and guided me in my stunned, utter disorientation to the safety of our barracks bunker during my first enemy attack. Bill also was instrumental in helping sort out the "CF" (Cluster Fuck) we had during our "Red Alert" Drills in August 1968.

David Morales -- SP4 who operated the mimeo and published our newspaper. Good guy, hard worker. When I was upset with someone or something, I had the doltish habit of using an inane pet phrase, "Bite my ass." Dave was walking alongside me one day. We paused to clear our weapons just before entering the Orderly Room and in response to something trivial or sarcastic he said, I repeated my "catch phrase." Dave quickly leaned closer and actually bit me on the cheek. "That the ass you mean?" he chided. I never used that phrase with him again.

SP5 Dick Lytle – a friend who worked in S2 and also was a great writer who often penned columns about politics and information coming out of Washington. We stayed in touch after we left the Army and Lynne and I visited Dick and his wife, Jackie in Elizabethtown, PA, not far from Lynne's parents' home in Wrightsville.

Sergeant First Class Louis R. Navarro -- had a pet monkey - another no-no for most troops. He also set up his own little (illegal) "PX." The closest official PXs were located at Camp Enari, the home of the 4th Infantry Division, and one at the Pleiku Air Force Base. We usually did not get to go to that one. Navarro's Little PX was on the second floor of the hootch next to ours. It consisted of two separate mini refrigerators with chains and a series of padlock across the front. Each of the locks was separated by two chain links. For a certain monthly fee you could buy a key to one of the locks. One fridge had soda like Coke or Pepsi in it while the other had beer … another item that generally was frowned upon in the barracks. Somehow Navarro got away with it. (He picked up his supplies via trips to the PX and by bartering with our scrounger, George Kondor.)

A significant reason a lot of GIs went to the PX was to buy beer by the case. For me, this did not happen often because I simply had no place to store it and it didn't hold well in the heat and humidity of Southeast Asia. So, if a few of us went together to buy a case for a special occasion like a birthday, it had to be consumed fairly quickly. There were times you could buy Vietnamese "Ba Moui Ba" – Biere "33." I hated that beer. To me it tasted like sand; at least that's the odd way I described it in one of my notes to Lynne. But my drink of choice wasn't beer back then. When I could get it at the LAS Club, it was Old Overholt Rye Whiskey on the rocks — or once in a while, mixed in an Old Fashioned.

Chapter Twenty

"Cupid (Draw Back Your Bow)"
Sam Cooke
(Written by Sam Cooke - 1963)

Leaving Vietnam

Eventually, my work and my having a Top Secret Security Clearance might have been instrumental in helping me get my next and final Army assignment. I was given the opportunity to request a specific posting for the last 10 months of my enlistment—although my request came with no guarantee it would be granted. Most, if not virtually all other assignments simply were made by the Army as they sought to fill areas of need around the world, especially for signal unit guys.

My initial thought was to request either Germany or California. I chose the latter and, as mentioned in the letter to Lynne, was fortunate to be assigned to the Combat Developments Command Experimentation Center (CDCEC) at Fort Ord, CA. This base was a training facility and also a place where new, top secret weapons, guidance systems, and communications equipment were tested. I worked there as a journalist for several months, then eventually became the NCOIC (non-Commissioned Officer in Charge) of the Information Office for 5 of the last 10 months that I was stationed at Fort Ord. CDCEC included a portion of the base near Monterey and extended to Hunter-Liggett Military Reservation south of Big Sur, plus Camp Roberts just north of Paso Robles.

I got to see some of the classified equipment that was undergoing testing, but my primary job remained focused almost exclusively on human interest news stories about soldiers in the units assigned to CDCEC. My stint as NCOIC came at an odd juncture in these final few months. That's when my predecessor, Sergeant Wolfgang Scherp, was transferred. Just a few weeks after that, our CO, Colonel Landry, also was moved to a different position. Those moves left me in charge of the entire CDCEC information operation, overseeing three other reporters: PFC Tommy Miller, Sp5 Bill Gates, another Private First Class (unfortunately I forget his name), Army photographer Sp5 John Wilson, plus a civilian office worker Maggie__ who copyedited our news releases. My job was to assign these guys to stories in and around CDCEC and at our other two bases. (And I apologetically affirm, we wasted a lot of time playing table-top "matchbox football." Ah, the leisurely life of the "newsroom"! After what I had just endured in the previous 12 months, I felt no guilt.) In all honesty, much of the "hard news" regarding what the folks at CDCEC were working on came from higher up the Chain of Command so we spent many hours trying to work up unclassified human interest stories such as "Two CDCEC Soldiers Extinguish Roadside Brushfire in Salinas," and the like. One of my stories, "Peace Corps Worker," made the front page of the October 16, 1969, *Seaside Post*. But that story was *not* about me. With this lead, "The transition from a primordial African society to the well-disciplined ranks of the United States Army is enough to make one's head spin," it had to be someone else.

And so it was. Private Jerry Hart from Madison, WI, was a clerk in the Instrumentation Support Group's Pictorial Branch of CDCEC who had served as a Peace Corps Volunteer in Somalia prior to being drafted. My bylined article went on to describe details of the work he had done and the experiences he underwent – even to being stranded in the desert for nine days!

Thus, after Vietnam, this assignment for me was an incredibly "soft" job. I worked only 4 and a half days a week, taking off either Friday afternoon or Monday morning, thereby making almost every weekend two and a half days. It was a marvelous way to wrap up this rather difficult time in my life. And, with the mild California weather, I was able to ride a small Honda motorcycle to and from work in laid-back-late-60s "Cali-style."

The Army provided on-base housing for Lynne and me in a comfortable two-bedroom home that had authentic, solid wood, parquet floors. It was located at the top of a hill at 226 Briggs Circle, overlooking Monterey Bay. The bay was visible from the small front yard and driveway of our house. Lynne and I were finally happy, living together in uniquely different and much, much better times.

My Windy Road

"Windy Road"
Denny Kaltreider
(Written by Denny Kaltreider - 1966)

My first novel, *Tears of the Virgin,* published in 2017 was an annotated transcript of the actual journal I kept during the two years I served as a Peace Corps Volunteer in Colombia, South America 1964-1966. In that book I detailed my day to day activities, special events, celebrations, and holidays. I also included a number of poems and expository writings I had written while there. Many were written by flickering candlelight or the soft glow of a lantern in the long, isolated, solitary hours during my first year in the jungle. Even though I had made friends in Nilo, there was nothing to do in the village after dark; there was no electricity to illuminate buildings or to run machines. "Night life" in the village was little more than sitting around a fire and chatting. (Actually we "hunkered" down in a squatting position, occasionally for hours at a time until the fire faded into a few glowing embers.)

Windy Road, the memoir you are about to finish reading, was cobbled together in a relatively similar fashion. Although I did not keep a journal during my 3 years in the military, I did write frequently to my wife, Lynne, who faithfully stored away and safeguarded those poignant notes and musings. Hence, in the course of compiling these memoirs, I read and reread, and now herein have quoted and commented on those 260+ letters, adding details or clarifications as appropriate. Lynne saved these dated and individually numbered epistles in an old shoebox (sounds like a scene from a movie) from the time I entered training at Fort Knox, until the day we, together, completed "our" military odyssey at Fort Ord, California, October 30, 1969.

Except for significant events that impacted the course of my journey, I've chosen *not to include* nearly all of the content I wrote to Lynne in the nearly 150 letters sent from my time at Fort Knox. To anyone other than Lynne or me, they would be mushy, droll, repetitive statements of love and desires, frustration and the joys of being in love; some letters poetic, others simply unintelligible to the casual reader. Therefore, you have read only relevant quotes (along with a few poems) that reflect our relationship, what I was doing, or comments which I believe are insightful of my mindset during this difficult period in both of our lives. Likewise, I gleaned information and quotes from an approximately 110 letters, notes, and cards I wrote to Lynne while I was actually stationed in Vietnam.

And, finally, now more than a year after reading through these epistles and beginning to organize all my notes and information into something more organized, I discovered another secreted stash of letters sent to me by Lynne while I was in Vietnam. I thought virtually all of these had been destroyed. Indeed, many of the letters Lynne wrote to me were destroyed during Tet. Yet, somehow about 100 letters that followed those awful weeks did survive. This "new" find also includes letters and cards from my family, a few from friends in South America, two from buddies who had DEROS'ed back to the states from Vietnam, and several in-country communiques from colleagues remaining in Saigon. Yet, as much as these letters have helped to fill in a few of the gaps in my memory, some have opened even more intriguing and unsolved mysteries about my work and time in Southeast Asia.

During Tet the Army cautioned us not to leave letters with addresses and personal information lying around for fear our personal information might be compromised and our families targeted. During one period of repeated shelling, we were directed to burn "old" letters and correspondence from home, or at least destroy the return addresses, lest it fall into enemy hands if we were overrun. I'm glad to say that did not happen and a significant number of letters did survive.

Finally, to verify events that I describe in this memoir, I reread articles from *The Unicorn*, the unit newspaper I edited and published for the 43rd Signal Battalion, Pleiku, Republic of Vietnam. Nine hundred copies of these were printed and circulated at the end of each month during my "Tour 365" as the Army called it. I carefully examined a map of Vietnam I had marked with notes during my tour, indicating the places I visited or was sent on assignment. I also consulted at length with friends from the 43rd with whom I am still in contact. They provided much support and helped corroborate some of my recollections, filling in some details I had blocked out of my conscious mind.

Last, as I did in writing *Tears of the Virgin*, I sorted and sifted through hundreds of slides and photographs I took in Vietnam, many of which were inscribed on the edges and backs with detailed descriptions of my less-than-idyllic adventure. I have included a few of those photos along with brief descriptions of what they depict at the end of this book.

Perhaps the contents of my letters to Lynne might better be understood with the consideration that just two years before --- at the relatively callow and inexperienced age of 18 -- I had embarked on an overseas assignment, was figuratively and literally thrust alone into a tenuous situation my first year (in the jungle no less). I scrabbled my way out of that, then successfully worked my way into a position of relative significance, ultimately ending up as an on-campus Field Coordinator for Peace Corps Training at Brandeis University, Waltham, MA, during the Summer of 1966.

Coincidentally, on May 12, 1966, just prior to that assignment at Brandeis, Peace Corps Director Jack Vaughn sent me a letter, inviting me to go to Micronesia to help set up another new Peace Corps program, but I respectfully declined his invitation. I was ready to move on with my formal education ... or so I thought. Yet, within a year or so -- following those misty-eyed, idealistic twenty-six months in the Peace Corps, I once again found myself totally immersed in an entirely different and mentally, emotionally exhausting situation, one that was more than ever ... a matter of life and death.

I had been tempered and molded appreciably towards maturity by my experiences in South America. But I was also "adrift" in several ways - especially on an emotional level. And while I had made dozens, if not hundreds, of new friends, my heart was longing for something — better yet, *someone* — who might provide a firm foothold from which to continue my life. I found that exceptional person, the person I would marry within a year – Dorothy Lynne Warfield. Lynne also was going through a difficult period in her life and together we formed an incredible bond of friendship, trust, and love that has endured much - yet continues to thrive - more than half a century later.

POSTSCRIPT

I began composing *Windy Road* after writing and publishing *Tears of the Virgin* in 2017. "Tears" was a documented chronicle of my South American adventure as the USA's youngest (18-year-old) Peace Corps Volunteer.

In both of these volumes that describe my tortuous odyssey, I've shared details about my feelings, my anger, my trepidation, and my angst. In both books, I've labored to express the succession of emotions I grappled with in these two major life experiences of-and-in both peace and war. What I have not previously divulged to anyone is what ultimately led me to where I am today and some of the things I experienced upon "coming home" after my five-plus years of service to our country. Until now, I have chosen not to share some of the troubling episodes that have crept into my consciousness more recently.

In October 1969, Lynne and I departed California and returned to central Pennsylvania where I began classes anew at Penn State. I enrolled as a freshman student and Lynne continued work towards her Master and Doctorate degrees.

Our nation was in upheaval. Soldiers returning from battle - weary, wounded, and simply worn out - were being heckled, harassed, and spit on. We were accused of being baby killers, rapists, and murderers. Suddenly we had become the enemy ... despised and disrespected in our own country!

Anti-war and anti-government protests marred normally tranquil campus life while riots darkened the streets of our nation's major cities. Political figures and leaders of the anti-war movement, champions striving for equal rights for all people and advocates for improving race relations, Dr. Martin Luther King and Bobby Kennedy both were assassinated. After repeated denials, President Nixon was forced to admit that the war indeed had expanded into Cambodia, something some of us already knew but could not acknowledge. That last escalation led to an increase in the public's overall negative sentiment about the war, and the heretofore relatively peaceful protests against the war turned deadly. Then on May 4, 1970, four students protesting the Vietnam war were shot and killed by National Guardsmen at Kent State University. How the hell was I supposed to fit into this turbulent mess?

Simply put...I didn't; at least I didn't as a returning GI. Instead, I put on the mantle of silent bystander, meek protestor. And, in fact, as a subtle personal statement of defiance, just a few months prior, Lynne and I surreptitiously fitted a round, two-inch metal peace symbol into the shutoff valve on top of the water heater in our home on base at Fort Ord.

Back on the Penn State campus, Lynne and I stood by and watched as local student protests took place. I steadfastly remained silent about my past except for sharing stories about my Peace Corps experience. I said virtually nothing about Vietnam or my time in the Army. I did not join any support groups or organizations. The few meetings I quietly observed left me with a feeling that I did not belong .... anywhere. Ultimately, I chose to ignore all of the military-related groups and only joined the RPCV (Returned Peace Corps Volunteers) "Friends of Colombia" group in Washington, DC. Over the years when people asked about my time in Vietnam I routinely replied with a canned response, "I was an Information Specialist and photographer" ... and sometimes, "I don't talk about that," ofttimes with a disdainful look or a nominal and negative shake of my head.

I pushed my Army life into the deepest, darkest voids of my mind and tried to block the worst parts from ever resurfacing again. I didn't want to talk about it; I chose to keep it hidden and tried to ignore it, simply dealing with it in my own ineffective ways. Nonetheless, fragments of it periodically forced their way into my personal life.

In August 2018, I had occasion to meet with my two very best, life-long friends from high school. Both of them were in the shit deeper in Vietnam and for longer periods than I was. One of them had recently (after 50 years!) been diagnosed with PTSD. He shared his deeply personal and gut-wrenching story with me and reading it moved me beyond words. Beyond raw emotions, it triggered my own memories and I began to recall a few more shards of my experiences. And every piece that resurfaced for me was tarnished and tainted with guilt.

Inside I was, and still am confused and burdened with constantly reemerging feelings of that guilt. What really was my role in all of this? Did I actually play any part at all? Did I do enough? Should I have not done whatever "part" it was that I did or didn't do?

While I had periodically mentally retraced and brooded over pieces of those memories for more than 50 years (while keeping them "hidden" from others), it was only after the August 2018 meeting with my friends that I felt compelled to face my long-time demons. The result is this book. I especially needed to revisit the moments that nearly cost me my life in Vietnam. My visions of that trip on the road between An Khe and Pleiku is especially troubling. In the past, I routinely minimalized it, treating it as if it were a joke, a funny story, an amusing anecdote. "I fell off a truck, and no one noticed." That was my way of coping. But, in reality it was far from funny. My body tumbled and skidded along the roadside, menacingly and distressingly clouded by dust. The road was lined with a nearly impenetrable dense, tangled, deep green vegetation and a literal wall of bamboo. That image has frequently come back to haunt me in a vision of vertical bamboo prison bars with no escape; the passing convoy of trucks rushing by in a blur, everyone oblivious to who I was or why I was there on the side of the road; no one slowing down or stopping to help.

Likewise, the truck convoy and ambush in which my friend Donnie and several other colleagues died is grotesquely indescribable and that too has left an indelible stigma which I cannot erase.

I am proud that I served my country, but I am also introspectively conflicted about having done so. And there are times my service felt as if it were simply a complete farce, a real-life reenactment of Joseph Heller's novel, *Catch 22*, or Richard Hooker's book, *M*A*S*H*.

Over the past 50 years, I established a credible façade that not even my caring and loving family could penetrate. That disguise was antithetical to the internal disquietude I've kept masked and suppressed for these decades. Lynne says that I was "different" when I came home. Unfortunately, I was. I still am. And I forever will be.

I ask myself now if recounting this contorted and meandering story will somehow subdue my deep and overwhelming, dark and sometimes disturbing emotions? Or, will I continue to wrestle with the reemerging burden -- survivor's guilt -- that, somehow or some way, I didn't do what I should have done? Will I continue to wrestle with why I maintain this pretense and am not the person I appear to be to others?

I traveled from jungle on foot and by horseback - to city on foot and by bus – back to the jungle again, this time by helicopters, jeeps, and trucks - and finally to the sidewalks, paths, and roadways of what should be a more normal life, but I still wonder …..

and I still question …..

and I still weep silent and bitter tears …..

but these tears are no longer *Tears of the Virgin*.

Appendix

The photograph of the sentinel on the cover of this book as well as all the photos on the next few pages were taken by me during my Tour of Duty in the Central Highlands of Vietnam.

December 1967 – December 1968.

> Helicopter overview of our area looking south towards the city of Pleiku and Dragon Mountain (right-rear in distance). "Tropo Hill" communication screens left-center, Company A barracks (closest to screens), HHD 43rd Signal Brigade compound to right-center across the dirt road. The "Dust Devil" (left) is swirling near the northwest corner of the 71st Evacuation Hospital which was located slightly over the rise behind the screens.

The author (on the right) and friend, Dave Clemens (left). This is one of our "rides," a Huey from 41st Signal Group based in Qui Nhon.

Approaching landing area 43rd Signal Compound, Kontum. Our co-pilot is seen in this photo which was taken from my typical position behind pilot and next to starboard (right door).

Huey landing at Company C Compound;. Photo taken from guard tower.

140

Left top photo: buildings across road from C Company Compound in Kontum. Those buildings were taken over by VC-NVA & had to be blasted out by Spooky and the men of C Company, 43rd Signal Battalion during Tet. (I took this photo from atop/inside one of our Guard Towers.)

Center: ground level view of damage and graffiti on one of the buildings shown in photo above

Left: You can see how the gatling guns on Spooky plus shelling from tanks shredded the trees and roof of the building, reducing some to rubble during the fierce fighting of Tet Offensive.

Artillery (left) and fighter strikes (below) Photos taken from helicopter as we flew in behind these attacks

Below: Gas Station in Ban Me Thuot riddled with small arms fire during the Tet

The top two photos on this page were for the editorial I wrote (but not published) that nearly got me charged with an Article 15. Rolls of Razor Wire and spools of Concertina Barbed Wire are sitting by guard tower & bunker on our perimeter. Meanwhile, the CO had our men "beautifying the compound" and planting flowers outside his office. (small pic)

Me - posing by a "spider hole-tunnel" dug by Viet Cong under our perimeter wire. Tunnels were used to infiltrate many compounds. This tunnel was located just beyond the uninstalled barbed wire in photo above.

POW Camp near Pleiku

143

Dak To
April 1968

Pleiku Street
Vendors & Market
(middle photo) and
downtown Pleiku
(bottom)

Dedication of school partially funded and built with assistance of men from the 43rd Signal Battalion

Inside one of the classrooms

Playing Duck-Duck-Goose under watchful eye of RVN guard

Preparing a site for a home to be rebuilt with help from men of 43rd Signal Battalion in Pleiku

LTC Leo DuBeau greeting owner of one of the rebuilt homes near Pleiku

Montagnard resettlement camp & Montagnard kids

Local, homemade, all-purpose transport

Driving cattle across road north of Pleiku near Montagnard village

At my desk in the "new" 43rd Signal Battalion Info Office, Pleiku 1968

During my tour I took hundreds of photos of men and women, civilians and military personnel, ceremonies, VIPs, Civil Action activities, landscapes, human interest scenes, the destruction of buildings during Tet, Air Strikes and Artillery Strikes, Viet Cong POWs, and a myriad of other subjects. By far, the most poignant photo I took was of this little girl squatting behind a barbed wire fence north of the city of Pleiku. It was not set up or posed; I simply found her in this position by the side of the road. Who she was and what she was doing here while other children played in the village nearby, we'll never know.

Windy Road

Windy Road, travelin' on; where do you lead, tell me where I'm goin'.
Windy Road, movin' on, tell me something, where do I belong?

First a brook, then a mill, goin' o'er another hill
Windy Road, windin' on,
someday soon, I'll know where I am goin.'

Secondly, a dove I see, flying oh, so gracefully,
midst the storm and tempest strong. Be my guide the whole day long.

> Feels like I've been travelin' along this road a million miles or more
> Been through sunshine, been through windstorms and pourin' rain
> Now it's time to head back where I started from.
> Windy Road take me home. *

Third there is a rainbow bright, lighting up the black of night
Showing me the way to go,
showing me the right one I know.

Windy Road, travelin' on; where do you lead, tell me where I'm goin'.
Windy Road, movin' on, tell me something, where do I belong?

Original 45 RPM recorded Sunday, October 30, 1966 at Deppen Studios, Windsor, PA

*I added the bridge to my original composition in 2019.

Lynne and Denny
November 25, 1967

Lynne and Denny
March 24, 2019

Other Books by Dennis L. Kaltreider available on Amazon.com:

Tears of the Virgin, 2017
Conversations with My Father, 2020

Made in the USA
Monee, IL
25 May 2020